HOW TO FIND YOUR *Perfect*
Golf Swing

HOW TO FIND YOUR *Perfect*

Golf Swing

DISCOVERING HOW TO PLAY YOUR BEST

Rick Smith

BROADWAY BOOKS

BROADWAY

Broadway Books titles may be purchased for business or promotional use or for
special sales. For information, please write to: Special Markets Department,
Bantam Doubleday Dell Publishing Group, Inc., 1540 Broadway, New York, NY
10036.

BROADWAY BOOKS and its logo, a letter B bisected on the diagonal, are
trademarks of Broadway Books, a division of Bantam Doubleday Dell Publishing
Group, Inc.

Library of Congress Cataloging-in-Publication Data

Smith, Rick, 1957–
How to find your perfect golf swing : discovering how to play your best /
by Rick Smith. — 1st ed.
p.   cm.
Includes index.
ISBN 0-7679-0123-1
1. Swing (Golf)   2. Golf.   I. Title.
GV979.S9S54   1998
796.352'3—dc21   97-45941
CIP

Book design by Chris Welch

98 99 00 01 02 10 9 8 7 6 5 4 3 2 1

To my father Jerry, for his genuine sincerity, constant support, and work ethic; my mother Nat, a true fan of the game, for her creativity and unconditional love; and my brother Andy, for developing my competitive spirit and being my closest friend.

To my beloved son Hunter, for whom I hope that life's journey brings him good health, happiness, and peace in all he does.

To Tricia, forever my sunshine.

I would also like to thank all the tour professionals that I have worked with, especially Lee, Roc, and Billy, for sharing their thoughts and bringing motivation, challenge, and friendship to my life.

Finally, I ask all golfers to bring respect and dedication to this, the greatest game, and to remember to have fun and appreciate the beauty that surrounds them.

Contents

Acknowledgments   ix

Foreword by Lee Janzen   xi

Introduction   1

Chapter 1   "Your" Golf Swing: The Seven Areas That Influence the Quality of Your Motion   5

Chapter 2   The Golf Swing's Most Important Position   53

Chapter 3   The Backswing   68

Chapter 4   The Downswing   88

Chapter 5   The Through Swing   99

Chapter 6   Preswing Fundamentals   111

Chapter 7   Ten More Yards   131

Chapter 8   Swing Faults, Causes, Corrections, Pitfalls   147

Chapter 9   Reflections and the Lessons I've Learned   177

Acknowledgments

I would like to thank Henry Young, my close friend and instruction associate, for sharing his knowledge throughout the many years on what makes a good golf swing work. With my busy schedule, without Henry this book would never have been written. We have consulted almost daily for many years. He knows my teaching more than anyone. In my opinion, he is one of the finest teachers in the country.

I also thank John Andrisani, a fine golf writer, whose editing and coordinating skills make this a helpful guidebook for players around the world.

I'm also grateful to photographers Leonard Kamsler and Nile Young, Jr., plus artist Allen Welkis, for their wonderful work that makes the instruction easier to follow.

Bill Shinker and Suzanne Oaks, of Broadway Books, also deserve thanks for believing in this project, brought to them by my literary agent, Scott Waxman.

Foreword

Golf is a multifaceted game. It involves the physical elements that dictate how you swing and mental elements such as the preshot routine that dictate how you visualize the correct shot before you swing.

Golf is also an individual sport, but each successful player needs a strong support team to succeed. I happen to be very lucky in the team area. I'm fortunate to have a wonderful family that gives me 100 percent support. I am also fortunate to have some good friends, most notably Rick Smith, who just so happens to be my swing teacher.

I have known Rick since age thirteen, when I first started playing golf. Right from the start of our relationship, I felt I could trust Rick, owing to his great knowledge of swing technique, his superb eye for spotting faults, and his strong ability to clearly communicate the instructional message.

Throughout my amateur and pro careers, I've been proud to have Rick around. He knows the swing better than anyone; so when mine is off, he quickly helps me put it back on track. Furthermore, when I come down the last few holes in a pressurized tournament situation, I don't need to worry about the complex variables of the golf swing. The simple swing keys of Rick's, that I've grooved over the years, allow me to hit good to exceptional shots virtually automatically. Most recently, this happened in the last day singles matches of the 1997 Ryder Cup.

Playing against Jose Maria Olazabal, the match was back and forth all day. However, suddenly I was two holes down with three holes to play. After surveying the scoreboard, I knew I had to win, or we (the American team) had no chance of taking the cup from the Europeans.

After winning holes sixteen and seventeen, I tied the match. But there was still the narrow, par 4 eighteenth hole to play. After a good tee shot, I needed to hit my iron shot close to the hole, from 158 yards out in the fairway. This is when Rick's tips on how to stay relaxed under pressure and make the perfect swing paid off. He taught me a swing I could have trust in. I hit a 7 iron shot 3 feet from the hole and scored birdie to win the match. Although the American team ultimately lost, I will forever think back and remember how well I performed in the heat of competition. After all, for a golfer, there is nothing more satisfying than hitting a pure shot under pressure. Rick has helped many other top PGA professionals. I am flattered when they ask him for a lesson, simply because it reconfirms my belief in him.

Rick has talked about a book for a few years, so I'm glad he's finally finished putting his thoughts down on paper. I know that many people will benefit from these writings. Although *How to Find Your Perfect Golf Swing* has finally been published, I probably won't spend less time with Rick. However, like you, I will have the benefit of reviewing his swing secrets any time I want.

Frankly, you won't learn to employ your own personalized perfect swing overnight. But if you follow Rick's instructions and repeat the correct movements and drills a number of times, you will give yourself the best opportunity to master the golf swing. So enjoy the book—the first time, and every time after that.

Good luck,
Lee Janzen

HOW TO FIND YOUR *Perfect*
Golf Swing

Introduction

Many of you play only a Saturday or Sunday game of golf or just hit a bucket or two of balls during the week. Yet you wonder why you are unable to improve your scores. Ironically, if you are like many other amateurs, you could practice and play daily and go backward, simply because of grooving faults.

In *How to Find Your Perfect Golf Swing,* critical elements of the swing, which are often overlooked, are discussed in detail. My hope is to give you some fresh insights into your swing so that you're able to make some significant, lasting improvements. This is not to say there are not other critical components to your overall game, such as the short game. However, in this, my first book, I decided to focus solely on the full swing. My hope is to share my thoughts on other areas of the game in subsequent books. The real uniqueness of this book is to start your learning process about the swing at a different point. Rather than first discussing the basics of the setup, I will cover the vital impact position first. The reason: If you know where you want to go, it's easier to get there.

Even the greatest golfers in the world take lessons. Jack Nicklaus, whom I was fortunate to work with, learned from Jack Grout. My other students have included Lee Janzen, Phil Mickelson, David Duval, Vijay Singh, Billy Andrade, and Rocco Mediate. David Leadbetter coaches Nick Faldo and Greg Norman to name just a couple of elite students. Butch Harmon is Tiger Woods's instructor. The list goes on, proving one point: All golfers need help.

In your quest to improve, you must understand that no top pro could play as well using a fellow pro's technique. For example, John Daly couldn't play golf as well as he does using a technique like Lee Janzen's, and vice versa. Jack Nicklaus would never think of copying Arnold Palmer's swing. Greg Norman would never emulate Fred Couples's action. What's interesting, however, is all these swings share a few certain common denominators. It's up to you to discover your own perfect swing, one that matches up with your physical strengths and flexibility capabilities and one that you know so well that when it doesn't work to maximum efficiency, you can identify faults and fix them. Your personalized swing can even be a little unorthodox, provided it enables you to return the club squarely to the ball at impact and produce powerfully accurate golf shots.

Many golfers work hard on their games with limited or no success. Maybe you are one of those golfers who practices hard, but goes nowhere. If that's the case, like so many of the other twenty-six million golfers in the United States, you probably look for quick fixes or tips that you think will turn your game around instantly. Going down that road, looking for the quick fix to cure your own swing faults, is not a sensible strategy.

In trying to find your own individual perfect swing, it's necessary to identify all the factors contributing to its deficiencies, as Ben Hogan, Sam Snead, and other superb ball strikers have done. I'll help you do that, because if you don't identify all the factors contributing to the makeup of your swing, there will be only superficial improvement. This *total* approach philosophy requires some effort on your part, but it's honest and realistic.

I'm not a quick-fix teacher; I look at the swing as a whole. Yet I'm not considered a method teacher either. I also understand that some of you simply can't employ certain movements of the swing, so throughout this book I offer physical exercises and drills that will help you increase your strength and flexibility. I also show you how to tweak your swing so that you are able to put the club in the best possible positions and hit the ball consistently more powerfully and accurately.

If you follow the instructions presented in this book—everything from the swing elements in Chapter 1 to the lessons presented in Chapter 9—you will become a complete golfer who intellectually understands the intricacies of the swing. More important, if you work hard, you will reach your goals of developing an easy-to-repeat swinging action and lowering your handicap through accurate shot making. No golfer asks for anything more.

"Your" Golf Swing

THE SEVEN AREAS THAT INFLUENCE
THE QUALITY OF YOUR MOTION

In order to improve your golf swing, I believe it is vitally important to first identify all the factors contributing to its makeup; in general terms first and more specifically for your own individual swing later.

My thinking is that unless you cover all the bases, you probably won't be successful in making any degree of lasting improvement. If you are not aware of all the factors contributing to your swing problems, there will be only superficial improvement.

You will see that this approach, which to some may be temporarily discouraging, is honest and realistic. It is an approach that has been missing in many golfers' efforts to improve, and is precisely why so many work so hard on their golf swings with limited or no success. This approach will help you avoid or extricate yourself from the many traps and pitfalls I've found so many fall prey to.

I'm sure many of you instinctively sense what I am saying because you know something has been missing in your efforts to acquire a good golf swing. You sense your approach may be incomplete or perhaps unsound. I think that by reading this book, you will begin to see why.

Let's take a look now at all the elements that I feel contribute to the makeup of a golfer's swing. As we discuss them, see which areas you feel may be contributing to your own mistakes.

1. Human Instinct
2. Physical Condition
3. Misperceptions
4. Practice
5. Mental Approach
6. Equipment
7. Instruction

Until you have a thorough understanding of each of these areas, and examine your own swing within the parameters of each, you will not be able to pinpoint, and therefore will not be able to address, the reasons for your swing deficiencies. Consequently, you will not attain sound, lasting improvement.

Let's examine each of these areas individually, beginning with the tendencies you bring to the mechanics of your golf swing as a beginner—before you ever swing a club or hit a ball.

Human Instinct

Many professional athletes have worked on their golf swings with teaching pros. And almost without exception, whether they are hockey, football, baseball, or tennis players, their golf teachers will tell you how these athletes regard the correct striking of a golf ball as one of the most difficult things to do in all of sports. In fact, even some of the world's best golfers, tour players themselves, would tell you the same thing. Why is this? What is it about hitting a golf ball consistently well that is so inherently difficult for so many?

Let's begin at the beginning. Before you ever held your first golf club, you had natural inclinations toward the mechanics of a swing. Unfortu-

Hitting a golf ball powerfully and accurately is an unnatural action that takes practice to perfect.

nately, many of them were wrong. Everything you do that feels natural and comfortable when you first take club in hand is probably contrary to correct technique. In other words, the mechanically sound swinging motion of a club is totally contrary to most of our innate tendencies. Even for golfers who look as if they were born with a club in their hands, correct technique is an acquired skill. It comes naturally for no one. There has never been a person who, when first taking up the game of golf, executed all the mechanics, from grip to setup to swing, correctly. Even little kids with wonderful swings, that you think are natural, usually learned through mimicry. Tiger Woods, for example, sat in a highchair and absorbed correct swinging motion by watching his father hit balls into a net.

Consider holding an implement such as a golf club. How many people do you suppose gripped a golf club correctly the first time they placed their hands on a club? If you said probably no one, I agree.

The grip directly influences the clubface's aim during the swing and, most important, at impact. If the golfer's natural grip is wrong, chances are the clubface position will be wrong at impact, sending shots left or right of the intended target. Because a player has no inclination to change a grip that feels natural to him, he is left with no other alternative but to adjust some other way; he is induced to modify the swing or aim to compensate. And if you understand these compensations are errors in themselves, you can also see how this is the genesis of a struggling, inconsistent golfer. Another grip element that relates to your swing is a natural instinct to hold the club too tightly, or over-control it. This fault promotes a violent striking action that's contrary to a naturally accelerated motion.

This, you might say, all sounds perfectly logical. Yet, on the other hand, I can't tell you how many students fail to realize the truth behind it. After being made aware of a certain swing flaw they ask, "Rick, why do I do that?" or "Why does that happen?" or "Why can't I stop doing that?" Just by the way they ask the question, the implication is that they want me to identify some immediately treatable symptom that will quickly eliminate the error. Usually this is impossible. The reason for the problem, and the answer to their questions, often is that it is simply their natural inclination. It is very deeply ingrained and often compounded by five, ten, or even twenty years of well-intentioned but flawed compensations. Consequently, they can be corrected only by a training process of some undeterminable length of time.

Let's look at another fault that is common to practically all golfers when they first swing a club. It is the familiar movement called *over the top*. Why do such a great percentage of golfers do this on the downswing? In my opinion, it is the natural, instinctive thing to do. It is an innate tendency that almost all golfers have as beginners and that most keep as they develop and ingrain their swings.

To illustrate how strong this tendency is, imagine a class of one hundred beginners of different ages, genders, and physiques. A group of qualified instructors teaches them nothing but proper setup, grip, and backswing. They are not allowed to make a downswing. Not one. Nothing is said about the downswing. Each student promises never to hit a ball and never to make a downswing during the program. Instruction continues until each and every student can execute setup and backswing perfectly with, say, a 5 iron.

At this point, each student, one at a time and unobserved by the others, is allowed to set up to a golf ball; make the backswing he or she was taught; and with continuous motion, complete the downswing with the intention of hitting the ball. How many of the hundred do you suppose would swing down over the top, outside-in? How many would exhibit other incorrect tendencies? Finally, how many would swing down absolutely correctly? It would be an interesting study. My feeling is that at least 85 percent would still swing down over the top, even though the setup and backswing were perfect. We would also see other incorrect natural tendencies, primarily an early uncocking of the wrists and/or a lack of shifting the weight forward, that are contrary to correct swinging motion. Both of these swing faults, by the way, are contributors to the over-the-top move.

Why is it so natural to swing down over the top? One reason is the innate *hit instinct:* This usually results in a forced movement of the club down with the right hand (for right-handed golfers) and upper right side. The correct sequence of motion is now lost, an early uncocking of the wrists occurs, and the upper right side tends to move out rather than down. The result: Over the top. A second reason is found in the very nature of the top of the backswing position. Unfortunately, the right side, arm, and hand are in a more dominant position than is the left side, making it easy to overuse these areas as the downswing is initiated. Another contributing factor is simply where the ball is. The ball, being on the ground and to the side of us, naturally induces us to go out and down to hit it.

Tour players have natural tendencies that are wrong, too, although few employ the over-the-top move at the start of the downswing. The difference, however, is that many pros know what their tendencies are and, therefore, can constantly monitor, adjust, and correct. You have to do the same. Do you know what your natural tendencies are? Do you know whether your grip is okay? Do you know if you have over-the-top tendencies and, if so, exactly why? These are fundamental issues you must confront and correct before any other mechanical problems, such as resultant compensations, are addressed.

The point here is not to discourage anyone, but simply to put things in proper perspective. I strongly believe that no matter what level of player you are, it is never too late to improve your swing. But to do so, you must approach it the correct way. You must first address inherent tendencies and correct them. This *can* be done using this book as your guide to improvement. Realize that the best players had swing problems early in their careers. Ben Hogan, probably the best ball striker of all time, had to revamp his setup and swing to cure a problematic hook shot. Nick Faldo evolved into one of the game's most accurate players, but only after spending two years changing his swing under the guidance of David Leadbetter. Tiger Woods has reached the top, in part due to Butch Harmon, who began helping Woods swing more effectively, starting in 1993. These examples show that eliminating wrong tendencies, or holding them in check, is achievable.

If you are a beginner, do not try to develop your swing without expert, professional instruction. If you are an athlete, don't assume being so will insulate you from having fundamental flaws in your motion or that they can be overcome by your athleticism. Furthermore, don't make the mistake of thinking expensive equipment will be the

It's never too late to improve your swing. But take my advice: Seek out a qualified PGA professional. Here I am working on my own swing with my friend and PGA instructor Henry Young.

answer. The right equipment can eliminate some needless problems (and at times can be of tremendous help), but it is not a panacea for all swing ills.

Rather, give the mechanics of the swing their just due. Let's make a commitment to attack any mechanical flaws with a level of effort equal to their importance. Let's identify and eliminate any of the wrong swing tendencies you have as a golfer so you can finally begin a process that will truly help you become a better ball striker.

If you truly want to improve, you must recognize some training must be involved. It will take some period of time to eliminate certain incorrect tendencies. So, please don't make the mistake of assuming once a problem is identified, there will be an immediate fix. Give it time. Don't get discouraged. You will have ups and downs before you improve permanently. Allow your body, your muscles, and your psyche an adequate period to replace old, natural tendencies with new ones that are more fundamentally correct.

Physical Condition

Thankfully, as we near the end of the 1990s, an increasing number of golf instructors are sensitive to teaching students according to the shape of the student's body and his or her natural strengths and degree of flexibility. Furthermore, many teachers are excellent at getting individuals with minor ailments (for example, knee and hip problems) to play good golf via simple setup and swing adjustments combined with a specific exercise program. The goal: To help students find the best swing that works for them.

Today, to play one's best, I'd say approximately 70 percent of the women I teach need some degree of upper body strength conditioning, specifically in the wrists, forearms, and fingers. With men, approximately 65 percent need to improve the flexibility in their upper torsos. Another 15 percent of the people I see have a minor physical limitation that influences their swing.

In regard to strength and flexibility problems, all my students are given simple, specific corrective exercises. For physical limitations such

Don't expect to be able to make a free, full turning action of the body unless you are physically flexible. Strive for flexibility, while short term, it's okay to adapt a setup and swing style that will give you the most success.

as knee problems, setup and swing modifications can be made. Usually, modifications can be done fairly easily, simply requiring flexibility and creativity in the instructor to make some compromise adjustments. These ailments need not be deterrents to improving a golfer's ability to hit a golf ball.

An example of how inflexibility influences swing technique can be seen in the golfer who is unable to turn the shoulders anywhere near 90 degrees. Or the arm swing may be very short, which keeps the club well short of parallel at the top. The common result is an over-the-top, outside-in downswing. Coupled with an innate tendency to do this anyway, the motion becomes extremely pronounced, resulting in pop-ups with the driver, shanks, tops, and low slices or bad pulls. If left untreated, flexibility decreases with age, but this condition can be slowed and even reversed.

Women who lack strength swing the club to the top much differently than those who lack flexibility. Because of the inability to support the club at the top, it moves into a low and overly long position. The insufficient height of the club and/or excessive length of the swing is the result of overbending the left arm (for right-handed golfers) and/or letting go of the grip with the last two or three fingers of the left hand. We might also see a severe collapse (bowing) of the left wrist with the dropping of the arms.

In an attempt to recover the club from faulty backswing positions such as these, the golfer instinctively starts the club down with the hands and arms. This is a compromise of the correct sequence of motion, as the lower body should be moving forward first, causing the arms and club to move down as a response. From my experience, this problem is almost always accompanied by an early uncocking of the wrists. The result: Most often an over-the-top move or, at the very least, the extremely fat and thin shots when the ball is not being hit off a tee.

The bottom line is that physical limitations are often the cause of swing flaws. Recently, physical therapists and other experts have become versed in the biomechanics of the golf swing. These professionals can evaluate the golf swing with computer assistance and determine how efficiently you are using your body. A regular stream of articles on how to gain strength and flexibility appear in golf publications; and more and more teaching professionals are knowledgeable about this component of the ability to swing a club well. If you need help in this area, it is readily available on many different levels.

I would encourage you to visit a PGA teaching professional at one of the golf courses in your area. With his or her help, determine if you have a physical deficiency that is hurting your swing and learn some drills that will help you eliminate it. The good news: This usually can be done very quickly. A week or two of working on drills, just a few minutes each day, will make a world of difference.

For a start, I'll give you two drills: one for flexibility and one for strength. If possible, observe yourself in a mirror as you do them.

Flexibility

This drill can be done with or without a club, but preferably *with* one. Assume the address position, arms hanging down in front of the body. Grasp your left wrist with your right hand; the right thumb is on top not under the left wrist. Keeping your left arm perfectly straight, turn your shoulders and swing your left arm back and up slowly; the movement being similar to that of a golf swing. The lower body should be stable (right knee flexed, minimal hip turn), resisting the movement of the upper body. When you have gone as far as you can, use your right arm to stretch your left arm and shoulder a little more. Your shoulders will turn a little more, and you should definitely feel the muscles stretching in your left shoulder area. Hold for thirty seconds, rest a moment, then repeat the procedure twice more.

If your backswing is becoming shorter, if you have trouble turning, or if you just sense you are getting too tight or inflexible, this is a wonderful golf-specific drill. If you do this twice a day and a third time as part of your warmup procedure when you play golf or practice, you will be doing your golf swing a tremendous amount of good.

Grasp your left wrist with your right hand; then use your right arm and shoulder to stretch your left arm and shoulder. This will help you develop a stronger turn.

Strength

To increase the strength in your fingers, wrists, arms, and shoulders so that you're able to properly control a golf club during the swing, practice the following drill.

Step 1: Start with a 5 iron and place only your left hand on the club with a correct grip for golf. Extend your left arm horizontally in front of you with the club up in a perfectly vertical position.

Step 2: Starting from here, slowly rotate your arm to the right until the clubshaft is horizontal to the ground.

Step 3: Slowly rotate your arm to the left until the clubshaft is horizontal to the ground again.

Try to never let the shaft drop beyond horizontal. Do as many full

Strength Drill: step 1

Strength Drill: step 2

rotations as you can, until you acquire the strength to do ten consecutively. When you can do ten, gradually increase the speed.

Whether you are a left- or right-handed player, do the same exercise with both arms, not just the weaker. Always do fewer rotations with your stronger arm, however, so you can develop equal strength in both arms. The reason is simple: Golf is a two-sided game—not just a left-sided game as many players think.

Misperceptions

Finding and establishing your best and most efficient swing is often made more difficult than necessary because of misunderstandings related to proper golf technique. I truly believe that many golfers have, unfortunately, been hindered by misinformation they have received or perceived as they've tried to improve their game.

As I talk with my own students and hear their explanations of what they try to do in their swings and why, I am struck by the many erroneous thoughts and ideas that run through their minds. Ironically, some of these thoughts originate from age-old adages that seem to do more harm than good: *Keep your head down, Keep your head still, Keep your eyes on the ball, Take the club back straight, Bend your knees, Sit down to the ball, Keep the left arm straight, Turn,* and so on. Surprisingly, much of this conventional wisdom has unwittingly created or accentuated swing faults, because of the golfer's misinterpretation of what the advice really means or simply because the adage itself is wrong or conveys the wrong message or image.

For example, let's take the sayings Keep your head down and Keep your head still. Yes, the head should not come up in the backswing, but it should not go down either. Quite often, students will actually lower the head in the backswing, because they are so intent on keeping it down. When this happens, the left shoulder drops too much as it tries to turn back and, therefore, is unable to turn back as far as it should. The result: Reverse weight shift and incomplete shoulder turn. This causes an over-the-top, excessively steep downswing that results in tops, shanks, slices, and pop-ups.

Another problem with this phrase is that it doesn't say *how long* the head must stay down. In the through swing, the head must rotate and release and come up for the right side to release properly through the ball and for the weight to transfer completely to the left side. The release and rotation of the head forward and up begins just after impact, and the process continues until the arms and club have completed their motion, coming to a full finish. At this point, the head should be vertically above the left leg, with the body rotated fully toward the target. At the finish, the shoulders preferably are on a slight angle, so that the right shoulder is slightly lower than the left. This means the spine angle, established at address, has been maintained throughout the backswing and downswing. You must allow for a slight rising of the spine in the through swing. As this slight rising occurs, the head also rises. As the head rises, it moves forward and rotates toward the target; so in the finish, it faces the target with the rest of the body.

The player who overdoes the Keep the head down adage cannot possibly finish this way. As this golfer approaches impact, then moves through the ball, the right shoulder moves into the chin. At this point, the player has two options: (1) keep the chin riveted in place and pre-vent the right shoulder (and ultimately the entire body) from continu-ing forward to a complete finish or (2) let the chin (and entire head) rotate forward and up as dictated by the movement of the shoulder. Obviously, the latter is correct. Those who do the former end up with very little weight shifted to the forward leg, have a limited amount of body rotation forward, and are unable to completely release the right side through the ball. All of these positions have a direct influence, and a negative one, on everything that is happening at impact.

Likewise, the phrase Keep the head still, can create problems for golfers. Besides preventing the release of the head forward as described above, it can also have very damaging effects in the movement of the body in the backswing—specifically related to the shifting of weight. Depending on their setup, many professionals today actually move the head slightly to the right (anywhere from one to four inches) in the backswing. In modern teaching, this is not only acceptable but advis-able. This is actually how the weight is shifted. The weight of your body goes where your head goes. As the shoulders turn back, the head is allowed to move slightly right, so the upper body turns and moves over a point just above the inside of the right knee. The center of the head and the middle of the left shoulder will be approximately in line with this point. Some players, such as Nicklaus and Faldo, start with their heads cocked back, eliminating any need for backward movement as the swing is initiated. Yet, at the top of the backswing, the top of the spine is definitely angled away from the target and angled back from the lower spine.

Those who attempt to shift their weight in the backswing and keep the head still very often employ a reverse weight shift. Since the head is not moving back, the only other alternative in the attempt to shift is to move the right hip laterally to the right. The player who does this might even lift the left heel to encourage or accommodate the motion. Indeed, the pressure on the right leg and hip, and the fact the left heel is off the ground, may give the player the impression that he or she has shifted weight. But it is a false impression. In fact, more weight is actually on the left leg. As the lower spine and right hip move laterally right, usually the upper spine and head move left toward the target (and often down as well) in the body's natural effort to balance itself. The result is a top-

Tiger Woods could never make such a strong turn and solid weight shift action on the backswing if he didn't allow his head to swivel. Notice how Tiger's head position is angled. The message: Don't overdo the Keep the head still adage.

of-backswing position that has the upper body, and thus a predominate amount of weight, over the left leg, not the right. This is a classic reverse weight shift.

One of the most repeated sayings in golf is Keep your eyes on the ball, and it can be thrown in the mix here also. Often golfers will keep the head down too long and block the correct follow-through movement. These players are so intent on keeping their eyes on the ball, their eyes are riveted on the location of where the ball was after it has already been hit. The net effect is the same as if they were proceeding under the Keep the head down edict. And I might add, if these golfers were to take the saying literally, they would not be looking at a spot where the ball was. Rather, they would be looking at where the ball is—presumably in the air, flying toward the target! To do this, however, the head must release correctly, as previously discussed.

The phrases Take the club back inside and Take the club back straight can also easily be misconstrued. Inside? How much? Straight back? How far and for how long? Do the same words apply to everyone? And does everyone interpret them exactly the same? The answer to the last two questions is, obviously, no.

If you have been taking the club back too much to the inside, *feeling* as if you were taking it back straight might be good. However, in the literal sense, the club never moves on a straight line; it moves in an arc. So as it is moving back from the ball, it is ascending in the air and working inward from the target line simultaneously. It also is moving along a curved line. That's because the movement of the clubhead in a golf swing is circular in nature. If one actually succeeds in taking the club back straight, or even comes close to doing this, the club will be lifted too abruptly in the backswing.

The phrase Take the club back straight was intended just for the first few inches of the backswing. But that qualification usually gets lost in the shuffle, which makes it easy for some players to misperceive the entire plane of the backswing. In their minds, the plane becomes very steep, very vertically oriented, like a Ferris wheel. At this point, there is no chance the club will move back anywhere near the proper plane. Someone who takes the club back straight, or lifts it abruptly in the takeaway, may do well to think of taking the club back to the *inside*. But such a word is vague and subject to interpretation. The operative concept here is that as the club moves in as it goes back, it must also be moving up. It is indeed possible to take it back too much inside; and if you are not made aware of that fact, it won't be long before you are doing just that.

I think it is impossible to describe in words the precise, correct movement of the club going back—at least my vocabulary is insufficient—so that every golfer can relate and execute it properly. That makes me wonder how we can then use the simple phrases Take the club back straight and Take the club back to the inside and think of them as being anywhere near sufficient. They are helpful only on occasion, when relative to an individual player's specific needs.

Another problem area is in the body's position at address, specifically posture. I very rarely see a golfer with legs that are too straight; but much more frequently than I should, I see legs that are too bent. Why is this? In my opinion, it is because of the false impressions one can easily

get from an incorrect phrase such as Bend the knees. I never use the word *bend* in reference to the knees. I say *flex* the knees slightly.

The adage Sit down to the ball is another one I never use. And, frankly, I have an extreme distaste for it. If you follow its directive properly, there is little chance that you will do anything other than bend your knees excessively. I might interject here that if someone tells you to do either of these things, a very natural and appropriate response would be to ask, "How much do I bend and how far down do I sit?" Otherwise, how would you know? And do these phrases equally apply to all golfers, regardless of height, length of arms, leg length versus torso length, and length and lie of club? Obviously not.

Sit on a stool is another popular saying that is supposed to help achieve the correct posture and knee flex, but I don't see how. Wouldn't you need to know how high the stool is? Would everyone who hears that phrase correctly visualize the stool's height and, therefore, know how much he or she should sit?

Several years ago I clipped from a popular golfing magazine an article that was demonstrating what the author perceived to be helpful images. One of the images dealt with the Sit on a stool adage. It showed a well-known tour player in the address position with a driver. A stool was positioned just behind him, and the photograph caption said, "Sit on a stool." However, as you looked at the photo, you could see that the golfer was no more sitting on the stool than he was riding a horse. I show this to my students all the time to convey to them how easy it is to become misled. The posture of the golfer was correct; however, the stool behind him and the inference that he was sitting on it were not. Two months later, golfers who saw the photo may forget the visual but remember the words and, consequently, bend too much at the knees.

Incidentally, as I described the image in the article, did you wonder how tall the golfer was and how high the stool was? The critical importance of posture to the swing is discussed fully in Chapter 6. For discussion's sake here, however, it's safe to say, if you overbend your knees your posture will be incorrect.

Here are some golf sayings that can easily be misinterpreted by many players. Depending on a golfer's problem, they can be helpful. But, ironically, they have hurt more people than they've helped.

1. Keep the left arm straight.
2. Turn.
3. Lift the left heel.
4. Keep the left heel down.
5. Make a one-piece takeaway.
6. Cock the wrists.
7. Rotate your left shoulder under your chin.
8. Stay down.
9. Clear the hips.
10. Slide the hips.
11. Pause at the top.
12. Keep the right elbow close to or against your side.

Do you think there is room for misinterpretation or confusion with any of these sayings? Some are even contradictory. Allow me briefly to address some of these sayings.

1. **Keep the left arm straight.** Ideally, the left arm is straight at the top of the backswing, which is what this saying deals with. However, the arm doesn't have to be straight; a slight bending at the elbow is permissible. Furthermore, straight does not mean rigid, which is how many golfers interpret it. What should be avoided is a left arm that has bent so much at the elbow it approaches a 90 degree angle. The most important point of any discussion about the straightness of the left arm, however, is to say that it should be straight at impact. It is far better to have a soft left arm (slightly bent) at the top and then have it straight at impact than to have a rigid (or even straight for that matter) arm at the top and then have it bent at impact.

2. **Turn.** *Turn* usually refers to the body in the backswing: specifically the shoulders and, to a lesser degree, the hips. If you don't turn enough, chances are you are outside-in down. Work on flexibility and by all

Nick Price

Nancy Lopez

Here are three superior players demonstrating that it's okay to allow the left arm to bend slightly at the top of the backswing.

Lee Janzen

means try to turn your shoulders. But an equally common problem is turning too much too soon after initiation of the backswing. This focuses attention on the questions, Turn what, when, and how much? The shoulders really don't turn that much during the first part of the backswing. When the left arm moves up to horizontal to the ground, the shoulders will have turned only about 30 degrees of the full 90 degrees desired. In addition, such movement is in response to the movement of the arms, not the result of conscious effort. The hips are responding to the movement of the upper body and, therefore, have turned even less. Frequently, I will see a golfer so intent on turning, the hips and shoulders begin doing so abruptly—immediately and excessively—as soon as the backswing begins. The unfortunate result is a movement out of sequence and a body motion that forces the arms to take the club back too much to the inside.

3 and 4. Lift the left heel/Keep the left heel down. Whether the left heel comes up or not depends on the flexibility of the golfer and individual preference. Either can be correct. The issue here, however, deals

Thinking turn can cause you to overrotate the hips and shoulders on the backswing.

with the words *lift* (lift the heel) and *keep* (keep the heel down). Both imply conscious effort on the part of the player, independent of other factors. This is not correct. For an inflexible golfer to turn the shoulders correctly and sufficiently in the backswing, the left heel may have to rise; but both that it does so and to what extent are caused by prior movement of the body, not by a conscious effort to lift the heel. There is a significant difference. The heel, therefore, may get pulled off the ground as an effect of the golfer's desire to turn the shoulders sufficiently: He or she may not be able to turn without the lift because of lack of flexibility. A golfer who is supple enough to turn completely with the heel down but who artificially lifts the heel will invariably overswing at the top and lose all hope of an accurate, powerful swing.

5 and 6. *Make a one-piece takeaway/Cock the wrists.* I once had a student who had an extremely late wrist cock in the backswing. When the wrists finally began their hinging, it was insufficient. The entire back-

Unless you need to allow your left heel to lift to turn fully, leave it planted. Don't ever consciously lift the heel. Here, I make a nice turn while keeping my left heel on the ground, as I am fairly flexible.

swing looked contrived and artificial. When I asked him what he thought about in the backswing, his response was "a one-piece take-away." My response to him was, "Yes, that's okay, but when does the takeaway end and the rest of the swing begin?" For that question he had no answer. He didn't have a clear definition of *takeaway* in his mind. He was so intent on keeping everything "one-piece" it prevented the natural and full hinging of the wrists through an acceptable segment of the backswing. Conversely, often a student will ask, "When do I cock my wrists?" By the very nature of the question, I know he or she doesn't have the proper concept of how this should occur. You should never cock the wrists. Rather, the swinging motion of the club and the weight of the clubhead cocks them for you, which will most certainly occur as long as nothing is done to interfere with the accomplishment of the task. Such interference might come from excessive grip pressure, an incorrect grip, an overzealous attempt to control the backswing, a

Ideally, you shouldn't have to think about cocking the wrists. The swinging motion and weight of the clubhead cocks them for you if you allow them to feel oily, free of tension.

backswing plane that is too flat, or from exaggeration of the one-piece takeaway.

7. ***Rotate your left shoulder under the chin.*** This phrase is supposed to ensure a full shoulder turn in the backswing. The turn of the shoulders was discussed earlier, but let me assure you this thought, or even the accomplishment of it, will not ensure your shoulders will be fully turned—particularly if you start moving your chin down and/or left in the backswing, as many do.

8. ***Stay down.*** The adage Stay down usually applies to the downswing and through swing. Those who attempt to follow this directive are usually pulling up and away with their upper body at the finish. However, this is an effect of another problem—either the posture, the swing itself, or a combination of both. Most often, such golfers are over-the-top, outside-in swingers. This type of swing will often force the golfer up. It will not do you any good to tell yourself to stay down. You may indeed try to do so. But you will not succeed until you fix the real cause of the problem, which is the swing itself. Lower handicap players who are too inside on the downswing can also experience this raising of the spine as well. But again, it is the result of the swinging motion, usually, not vice-versa.

9 and 10. ***Clear the hips/Slide the hips.*** These sayings refer to the motion of the hips in the downswing, which is discussed fully in Chapter 4. The major problem here is that the average player who tends to cut across the ball and who, therefore, already clears the hips, or rotates them through impact, does so excessively. However, he or she is constantly hearing on television how the professional is working on this move or makes this move beautifully, and so on. The implication is that the average player would be helped by doing the same. This is incorrect. For the average player who slices, trying to clear the hips would only make him or her slice more. Thinking of sliding the hips would be more helpful. The idea of clearing the hips is more beneficial for the player who is too inside-out and tends to hook or push the ball.

11. ***Pause at the top.*** Again, the pause is not something you make happen, but rather it happens naturally as a consequence of a correct swing, it's pace and proper sequence of motion.

12. ***Keep the right elbow close to or against your side.*** People often get confused about when this should happen. The right elbow moves

The right elbow should be free of the body on the backswing, yet should be pointing downward.

away from the side throughout the backswing, at the top, and initially down. It is only when the downswing has been half completed that the elbow moves in against the side. Too often I see golfers forcing their elbow into the right side immediately during the takeaway then keep it there throughout the backswing, which makes the club come back too inside and the backswing too flat.

These are just some of the sayings to think twice about before adopting them as part of your swing. It is not to say they are always wrong. Depending on the nature of the golfer's mistake, indeed any one of them could be helpful. Here are some other phrases that can be misconstrued, but let me identify when they could also be helpful.

	Could be helpful if:
13. Extend back.	right elbow too close to side in takeaway
14. Extend through.	left arm chicken-winging at impact

15. Swing the club toward the target.	through-swing too left or right
16. Finish high.	follow-through is too low due to an outside-in swing path
17. Release.	for good player who has too much lag
18. Employ a late release.	for poorer player who uncocks prematurely
19. Take the club back slowly.	it is your nature to be deliberate
20. Hit against a firm left side.	left knee sags at impact
21. Rotate.	you slice and arms fold and separate at impact
22. Maintain a firm grip pressure.	writsts are excessively active in down swing
23. Maintain a light grip pressure.	wrists are too rigid in backswing
24. Keep your head behind the ball.	upper body moves laterally past the ball prior to impact

The obvious point I'm making is to be wary, careful, and inquisitive when it comes to golf's phrases, sayings, and adages. If you are taking lessons, make sure you ask for, and get, a satisfactory, understandable explanation for anything said that might be unclear to you or subject to interpretation. If you read something that is unclear, ask your professional for an explanation. You might also ask your teacher about the validity of certain concepts you might have heard about the swing. You may be surprised by some of his answers.

Practice

There are many drills and exercises golfers can do at home, or other places other than the driving range, that are wonderfully effective in improving one's swing. These drills are done without hitting golf balls and, in some cases, without swinging a club. Frankly, this type of training is *the* most productive at certain stages in the developmental or corrective process of one's swing. This idea is usually enlightening and encouraging to golfers who think they should be frequently hitting practice balls on the range to get better but who don't have the time or find it inconvenient to do so. In fact, for many golfers who are working on swing improvements, the club and the ball actually get in the way—deter progress—whereas motion training with a mirror allows them to control exactly what they are doing; ensures they are doing it correctly; and most important, allows them to equate the feeling of what they are doing with the motion they are actually making.

For inexplicable reasons, in golf, your feelings usually lie to you: What you feel you are doing and what in fact you really *are* doing are usually quite different. Working in front of a mirror allows you to see exactly what these differences are. That said, when you are playing your best and swinging the club with the greatest amount of ease, both mentally and physically, you will be doing so because you can relate to a certain *feel* for a good swing, not simply because you understand the mechanics of it and can execute a certain number of its positions.

Swinging in front of a mirror, without worrying about hitting a ball, allows you to check certain key positions.

A certain percentage of practice time, however, should be spent on the range hitting balls. My guess, though, is that 80 to 90 percent of amateur golfers who do this, do so incorrectly.

There is a popular recent saying that says practice doesn't make perfect—perfect practice makes perfect. If you are practicing wrong things, just jumping from one idea to another in a trial-and-error procedure, or trying out the latest magazine or TV tip, you probably are doing more damage to your swing than good.

To me, perfect practice means practicing intelligently. This professional approach ensures that you truly improve a flawed swing, rather than more deeply ingrain faults or make changes that are incorrect, causing you to compound your problems. Obviously, to accomplish positive goals, you must know what is truly wrong in your swing, and you must have a clear plan of what particular flaw(s) you will work on in any given practice session. The action should include working on specific ball-hitting drills that are designed to help you correct these flaws, and you should have a practice station that will help you assess your progress.

The first step, then, is correct identification of your swing errors. This process can begin with assessing your ball flight tendencies. Do you hit the ball too low or too high? Do you tend to hit pulls and slices or pushes and hooks when you hit a misdirected shot? Do you hit occasional pop-ups with your driver, or possibly a lot of low-heeled shots? What about your divots? Are they deep and going left, or shallow and going right? Do you hit a lot of thin shots with your irons and fairway woods, or possibly just a lot of fat shots? Or maybe a combination of both? As a lower handicapper who hits draws as the predominant ball flight, do you fight the occasional excessive hook or block with your driver? And what about your alignment and ball position tendencies? Have you been told more than once you aim too far to the right or left of target? Have you been told, or do you already know, that your ball position is too far forward or back in your stance? All this information is very revealing and, if correctly analyzed, can help you determine what is going wrong with your swing.

You can also get some insight into your swing from people you regularly play with; do you hear the same thing over and over? "Your grip is too strong," "Your backswing is too flat," "You overswing," "You reverse weight shift," and so on.

The next step is to corroborate such information by filming yourself, watching yourself swing in front of a mirror, or better yet, have a filmed lesson with an expert teacher who can confirm for you exactly what is right, what is wrong, prescribe drills, and if there is more than one fault, suggest what the order of priority should be as you begin the corrective process.

As you prepare to hit balls for drills or just to hit shots normally, there is one very important thing you should do before you hit your first shot: Set up a work station that is aligned to a specific target.

Having a specific target is a prerequisite for the work station, because its primary function is to ensure you are aligned correctly to it—to ensure that where you are looking and where your body is aimed are the same. If this is not the case, the direction of your swing and the alignment of your body will be in conflict and your swing will be flawed. Plus, knowing you are correctly aimed to a specific target eliminates one important variable as you assess a swing that has produced an errant shot. It eliminates the possibility of misalignment and places the fault squarely on the shoulders of the swing itself. To say it another way, if you don't know exactly where you are aiming and you hit an errant shot, how could you possibly know if the fault was in your aim or your swing. And if you don't know that, you very well may blame the wrong thing.

One way to establish a work station is to take a couple of clubs and lay them on the ground perfectly parallel to one another and a distance apart that represents the distance between the ball and your stance line with any particular club. The outside shaft points exactly to a specific target; the inside shaft represents the parallel line on which you want to place your feet. This line also is a reference line for the position of other body lines, primarily hips, shoulders, and arms. They should also be positioned parallel to the target line. This represents correct alignment of the body and is a position called *parallel left* for the right-handed player—so identified because the body lines, when extended down range, point left of the target—not to it. Since the body lines and target line (line of flight) are parallel to one another, only one can point to the target. A misperception is that the stance line points to the target. It does not.

As you hit balls, simply place them as close as possible to the target

One reason Tom Kite has played so consistently over the years, hitting a high percentage of fairways and greens, is because he practices intelligently. In fact, he was one of the first players on the PGA Tour to use a practice station; adding a third club, running horizontally, to help him get his ball position right. Here he is, in the early days, stepping into his practice station.

line shaft without risking the possibility of hitting it. As you hit more and more balls, constantly check the positioning of your feet, fighting any tendency to move them into a position other than parallel to the target line. Once you have correctly identified your preswing and/or swing deficiencies, you can use the drills that are specifically designed to correct them. My recommendation is that for every fifty balls you hit on the practice tee, a minimum of forty should be hit doing your various drills. The other balls should be hit with a normal swing. If you have several things to work on, it is important you work on them one at a time at first. If you try to make too many corrections at once you probably won't do any of them very well.

For example, let's say that you have four problem areas that need to be corrected: (1) your grip is too weak, (2) you take the club back too far inside, (3) your upper body hangs too far left during the backswing, and (4) you then swing down outside-in and hit shots that curve excessively left to right. After you have done body-motion drills and arm-swing drills in front of a mirror, you are ready to go to the range to hit some balls. After targeting each of your weak spots, you should have four or five hitting drills each specifically designed to counter one incorrect tendency. Instead of trying to fix all problems with every practice shot, hit ten balls executing one drill, ten more balls doing a second drill, ten with a third drill, and ten with a fourth. After hitting forty or so balls as drills, you should hit ten shots focusing on the feelings the drill swings have conveyed to you. If one particular problem area was more pronounced or less responsive than others, this area might require a greater percentage of drill shots.

Going back to the combination of faults I just mentioned, you could first work on your grip, hitting ten balls, teed up, with a 7 iron. Hitting good golf shots is not the immediate goal. What's important is allowing the hands to become accustomed to a new position on the club as a swing with a ball is made. That's why you tee the ball at first—to make it easier to hit. And, if you hit some poor shots initially, that's okay too. Be patient. Give your hands plenty of time to get accustomed to a new position. Your swing should be slower than normal, and if you feel more comfortable employing a half swing rather than a full one, that is fine.

After these ten balls, move on to another problem—say your overly inside takeaway. To cure this fault, put an old shaft vertically in the ground, opposite the ball of your right foot and far enough away that on your takeaway, when your club shaft comes up horizontal to the ground, the hosel of the club just touches the top of the vertical shaft. Next, tee up ten balls. Employ a slower than normal swing. Hit each ball, trying to make sure the shaft and clubhead ascend in the takeaway just to the left of the shaft in the ground. Getting someone to watch your swing and confirm the takeaway position can be very helpful. Again, your main focus for those ten balls should be the takeaway.

Another problem was the reverse pivot at the top. Use ten more balls to address this fault. From your mirror work, you should already have a feel for good body motion. In hitting each shot, you should key on your left shoulder, trying to move it over your right knee at the top. Alternatively, swing back to the top, stop, lift your left foot entirely off the ground, replant it, swing down, and hit the ball. Both these movements will ensure that your upper body is moving correctly over your right knee at the top, not hanging over your left. As you swing back, you should also be aware of your grip and your takeaway action. Still, you should be focusing most intently on your upper body position at the top. An ideal practice area has a mirror so you can check this vital position yourself.

Continue on, addressing each of your problems singly, in a certain order. Just for a change of pace, after completing the drills, hit ten or so shots normally, selecting one key thought for simplicity, and then focusing on the feel of the *entire* motion, not just a segment of it. Time permitting, start over and repeat the process. With practice, the different things you are working on start to be absorbed by your body. You are in a training mode, repeating a certain motion over and over so you can gradually begin doing it without thinking about it. This is called *habituating a motor skill,* commonly referred to as *muscle memory.*

Another thing you should do that can be very helpful is to establish an intermediate reference point along your target line. For example, place a head cover about seven or eight paces in front of your golf ball, exactly on an extension of your target line. This is an excellent visual reference for where you want the ball to begin its journey. Don't panic if this reference point looks too far to the right (or to the left, for left-handers) as you take your address position. This is an optical illusion called *parallax,* the result of your eye line being inside your target line, not on it.

As you hit shots, try to be aware where the ball starts relative to your intermediate reference point (and target), and then watch the flight of the ball to see if it curves. Again, these are clues to your clubhead path and clubface position at impact and provide vital information for you to be able to accurately assess the swing you've just made. One cautionary note for people who get the clubface excessively open or shut at impact: Because the ball reacts more strongly to the clubface position than to the path (about two-thirds to one-third), if you swing left with a very open face, the ball will not start left but rather will start straight or even right of target and go farther right as it curves. This is a very glancing blow that also causes the ball to fly a short distance. Be careful not to interpret the ball's movement to the right as a result of a swing in that direction. If you do, and swing more left, you will exacerbate the problem. The same thing, in reverse, would apply to the low handicapper who swings too much to the right (too inside-out) and closes the clubface excessively. Often he or she wants to swing more right because the ball is going left, but again, this is the wrong prescription for the problem.

As you practice, you should think of yourself as a detective who is constantly looking for clues that will help you correctly pinpoint faults and eliminate them. The flight and curvature of the golf ball are your primary clues. They tell you the clubface position and the direction of the swing at impact. Any ball that is curving in the air means the clubface is open or closed to your path. If the ball's initial flight direction is left or right of your target, you know your path most probably is outside-in or inside-out. This gets a little more difficult because the ball reacts more strongly to the clubface position at impact than to the path of the clubhead. Nevertheless, knowing where you are aiming and watching the ball's initial flight direction relative to your aiming point as well as its curvature reveal your primary clues.

There are a few other things that can be incorporated in a practice session as you move through different stages of your development. Better players should definitely work on curving shots in both directions as one of their drill procedures. Too many times I have seen good players get themselves into deep trouble with their swings because they have fallen in love with a fade or draw, and that's all they ever hit. But, pretty soon, the fade turns into slice or the draw turns into a severe hook or block to the right. The golf swing is very dynamic in the sense that it is always changing; the changes from day to day may be imperceptible to the eye or hard to feel, but before you know it, strange shots begin to appear. For the draw player, the minute changes, over time, move the swing too far from the middle of the scale. As a result, he or she ends up way down on the hook end, so to speak. And now, the draw player can't hit an intentional fade. This situation could have been avoided if the player hit a few fades each time he practiced, even though the draw is the preferred shot. In doing this, the golfer keeps the swing in touch with the middle of the scale, preventing it from naturally gravitating toward an extreme, which normally happens when he or she hits only one type of shot.

Another procedure that can be very helpful for all levels of players is to hit balls while imagining that you are on a particularly difficult hole that has you constantly boggled.

Often we allow ourselves the mental luxury of getting too comfortable in practice, particularly since the range area is around 150 yards wide. There are no out of bounds, water hazards, deep bunkers, and so on. Besides, if a shot is missed, there's always another ball in the pile to hit. As your swing improves, you reach a point in your development when practice time should be devoted not to the swing you make, but rather to the shot you hit. It's good to put a little pressure on yourself to hit a particular shot you have in mind, even though you're on the wide open range.

To do this, pick a shot that really challenges you. It might be a tee shot on a certain hole on your home course that is particularly tight: trees left, out of bounds right. Or it might be a hole that doglegs right and demands a supercontrolled power-fade drive. Whatever the situation, see the hole in your mind as you look down the range. Establish the borders of the fairway. Visualize the trouble. Imagine five hundred people are around the tee watching you. Now, hit your shot. If your imagination is good, you will feel some pressure. Is this good? Absolutely! You have to prepare yourself for this during a real game on the course. If your visualization capacities are good, you can put yourself in the same pressure situation on the practice tee. Keep hitting shots until you are confident you can perform—confident that your swing will not break down owing to the level of difficulty of the shot. Because of this practice, when you actually play the hole you imagined, you'll be ready. You will feel more confident you can pull the shot off.

Even if you don't succeed at first, stick with the practice procedure. You can still make a poor swing for various other reasons and not hit your best shot. But you don't want this to happen because of undue stress, anxiety, or pressure you put on yourself. You can play this game hitting a lob shot over a bunker, a pitch over a lake, a tee shot on the first hole of a tournament, or a fairway wood down a tight fairway. Practice like this is far more productive than hitting shots without intent or consequence.

A continuation of this theme would be to visualize playing an entire hole or holes, tee to green, as you hit balls on the range. For example, on a par 4, hit a tee shot with your driver, then take an iron out and hit it to an imaginary green. Next, play a par 5, by hitting a drive, fairway wood shot, pitching wedge shot. Simulating on-course play is a wonderful approach for your practice. It helps you bridge the gap between your practice tee swing and on-course swing, which many find difficult to do. When you're practicing, the tendency is to hit one shot after another, over and over, with the same club, which is a totally different routine from when you are on the course. I'm not saying it's wrong to do this on occasion. I'm simply saying a practice procedure you can adapt into your repertoire is to spend some percentage of your practice time simulating the playing of holes. I think you'll find it helpful in your preparation for on-course play.

I've cited a few examples of things you can do to make full swing practice time more productive. If you put your mind to it, I'm sure you can think of other helpful procedures. My point: Do not hit balls without a specific purpose. Practice in a manner that ensures you are spending your time wisely.

Mental Approach

As I mentioned earlier, executing a shot to the best of your ability during course play is a daunting task. The pressure of performing in front of others, the challenges presented by the course itself, and the self-imposed anxieties of trying to do your best and score, all tend to make the smooth, rhythmical execution of your best swing more than a little difficult. It would be nice if you had a procedure that would help negate or at least lessen the pressures and anxieties you may feel interfere with your ability to perform your best. It would be nice if you had a procedure that helped you focus correctly, concentrate correctly, so that the possibility of any anxiety-producing thoughts or situations would be greatly diminished.

In fact, there is such a procedure, although far too many golfers do not employ it or place enough value on its merits. The procedure is called the preshot routine; and when established and used on every shot, it becomes your best friend on the golf course. As such, its calming influence affords you the opportunity to make your best swing in the most pressurized of situations. The preshot routine encompasses everything you do after selecting the club you will use and then prepare to hit your shot, the twenty or thirty seconds immediately preceding the actual swing.

To the second, professional players do exactly the same thing in exactly the same amount of time every shot. Each player's routine may be a little different; but whatever it is, each follows it precisely. For example, Scott Simpson takes two full practice swings before each shot, standing to the side of the ball. In preparing to hit a tee shot, Greg Norman stares at the target for about five seconds, takes three practice swings from behind the ball, then steps into the shot. Other pros "waggle" the club a specific number of times before they swing.

Why is this such an integral part of a good player's procedure? He or she knows that the consistency of what is done before making the swing influences the psyche and conscious mind so that the physical action is getting the green light to proceed. The mind is telling the body all systems are go. It is a mental–physical phenomenon that can either be in sync or be in conflict.

We all have experienced the situation of hitting a poor shot and then thinking, or saying, "I wasn't ready to hit that shot." Somehow, instinctively, you knew all was not well before pulling the trigger. Your mind was not giving your body the green light. The light was still red, but you swung anyway. Your subconscious is always monitoring what you do as you prepare for your shot. If it senses you are proceeding in a manner that it is familiar with and at a pace it is familiar with, you are receiving signals of comfort and calmness. All is well. So far so good. Proceed with the swing. Pull the trigger. The mind and body are one and in total synchronization. Because the routine is consistent, it becomes so familiar to you that, as you enter into it, it puts you in a zone of comfort that helps you feel confident. The comfort comes from the familiarity. The confidence allows you to trust your body to proceed with the swing and trust also that the shot will be a successful one. It may not be, but you can be sure it rarely will be if you don't feel the comfort, calmness, confidence, and trust you create through a consistent preshot routine. If you are working on the development of your routine, as you go through the procedure and are consciously involved in each step, your mind cannot also be involved with negatives, such as: "Don't hit the ball in the water left" or "Don't hit the ball out of bounds right."

As you observe yourself going through a routine you will become aware of things like whether it feels better to take one practice swing or several. You will notice where you might take them, behind the ball or to the side. You will start your procedure at a specific point or location. Usually, and my recommendation is to do this, it begins from several paces directly behind the ball, on the target line. This is where you can best see your target line, visualize your shot, and see the alignment lines of your body. In any event, if you currently have no set procedure or go about the preparation for your shot in an inconsistent, haphazard manner, I suggest you change your preswing habits.

I think it can be very helpful to observe professionals and simulate the things they do that you sense you would want to incorporate into your own routine. Next, fine-tune the routine to your own liking. Work on this at the practice tee. Rehearse your routine, and get it down pat; then use it with every shot. Some of you may find it will also prevent you from thinking too much about the mechanics of your swing.

In practice, we get into a routine of hitting one ball after another with the same club and often get into a flow of hitting a lot of good shots. Then, as the saying goes, comes the longest walk in golf, from the practice tee to the first tee. Different environment, more pressure, greater level of anxiety. What are you to do?

The solution reverts back to the preshot routine—one that incorpo-

Most pros start the preshot routine from behind the ball, simply because it provides the best view of the target and the target line.

rates at least two, but no more than three practice swings. However, these swings should be done in a certain way for a specific purpose.

To simplify several mechanical thoughts a student of mine may be working on, I encourage the adaptation of a short phrase that incorporates all his or her changes. For example, let's say a student has been taking the club back too far inside the target line, then lifting it too vertically without a sufficient shoulder turn, followed by an over-the-top downswing with an open face at impact. After we go through all the explanations and rehearse the correct positions, I then create a phrase for the student to help him or her simplify the changes and get a flow going.

In this case, such a phrase might be:

Extend (straighter back takeaway)
Turn (turn shoulders 90 degrees)
Inside (approach ball with clubhead from inside the target line)
Rotate (extend both arms and rotate arms through impact)

Each word *(extend, turn, inside, rotate)* represents all the information conveyed to the student through the lesson, and the student has a thorough understanding of the entire physical motion each word represents. The short phrase activates the movement without the usual accompanying mental gyrations that tie so many golfers down.

With this short routine, you now have a bridge to cross from one side of the brain to the other. You have a procedure to get away from the mechanical thoughts that tighten the swing and detract from its flow. Instead, you create a mental focus that promotes a rhythmic swing. Even when doing this and missing a shot, as you will surely do on occasion, be confident in knowing this procedure will give you your best chance of executing good swings on a consistent basis with the least amount of mental effort.

You now have a procedure that, by its very nature of being done on a consistent basis, will encourage comfort through familiarity. This will help you deal with the heightened levels of anxiety experienced on the course. Within this procedure is a method by which you can learn to execute your best mechanics without thinking mechanically, even if you are in a stage of making significant changes to your swing. As you get better and better at this, you will gradually be able to trust your routine and your swing more and more. As a result, you'll eventually be able to swing the club correctly, without having to think about it. This is when the game truly becomes fun.

Equipment

Clubs can hurt you or help you, but will not make you or break you. Sure, clubs that are not suited to you can certainly hinder your progress and force you to make unnecessary and unwanted compensations. Keeping things in some perspective, however, I often think back to the wonderful golf played by the great players during the early part of the twentieth century, by Bobby Jones, for example, who won the Grand Slam using heavy hickory-shafted clubs.

We live in a technological era in which advances and changes to clubs are happening so rapidly it would be foolish not to enjoy their advantages. If you are in the market for clubs, the first advice I would give you is not to make a purchase without the guidance of a qualified PGA pro or other expert in club fitting.

As a beginner, you need the guidance of proper posture in the setup. This feature of technique establishes arm hang, hand position, and how far your hands are from the ground, which in turn influences the length and lie of the club. These are critical elements to a properly fitted set of clubs. Most people are going to fall into a "normal" range based on body type and stature. However, if you are taller or shorter than average or have an arm length that is shorter or longer than normal, you will definitely need clubs that are modified, both in lie and length. Grip size is another issue that relates to hand size, finger length, and in the case of some women, even length of fingernails. Generally speaking, grips that are too large hinder hand action through the ball and a feel for the club-head. Conversely, grips that are too small for the golfer encourage excessive or overactive hand action.

Another critical component of club fitting is the shaft, which is the engine that drives the club. In my opinion, many beginners and recreational players use a shaft that is too stiff, which makes it more difficult to get the ball in the air sufficiently, detracts from a better feel of the clubhead, and decreases distance when the swing speed is insufficient to cause the shaft to load and unload. This may well result in the player

Matching the right shaft flex to your swing speed and trajectory is a very critical element to consider when purchasing new clubs.

compromising his or her technique (for example, casting to try to help the ball in the air or produce more distance). This is also a critical issue for seniors who have lost clubhead speed since their more youthful days. Longer, more flexible shafts, allow the senior to load and unload a shaft at slower swing speeds.

I would not recommend you use a stiff shaft unless you have a minimum clubhead speed of ninety miles per hour. As you move into the realm of shafts you are really getting into an area that requires precision measurement. The tolerance for consistency (of shaft to shaft through a set) and the match (between shaft characteristics and golfer) are of paramount importance. Consistency of shafts through a set involves flex, torque, kick point, and overall weight. The many variables in shafts have really created confusion in the marketplace, even, surprisingly, among tour players. It goes without saying the recreational player must have professional guidance in this area, just as tour players do. They have access to all the top shaft companies at each tour stop, giving them the opportunity to try out different shaft characteristics until they find just the right one. You, too, should not buy clubs unless the seller has a wide variety of demonstration clubs with several different shafts for you to try. Hit enough shots with various types of clubs until you have sufficient opportunity to make a valid assessment.

Getting back to shaft characteristics, if your swing speed is slow and you hit the ball under 235 yards off the tee, a higher torque may help you. In addition, a lower kick point should help you, along with a medium flex and a lighter weight.

Keep in mind that although the shaft is the club's engine, the weight of the head plays a major role in the shaft's characteristics. Because of lighter head and shaft materials, club makers have been able to make bigger heads and longer clubs. Bigger heads are definitely advantageous, because of perimeter weighting and larger sweet spots. While I think that iron heads (and those of fairway woods) have reached their maximum size because of other variables such as rough and tight lies, driver heads probably will get even bigger owing to advances in alloys and the advantages of perimeter weighting. Because the ball is on a tee, the same restrictions for irons do not apply to the driver.

In regard to driver length, how long is too long? Because of the golfer's fascination with distance, club makers are doing all they possibly can to fulfill this desire. Remember, however, as you strive for more distance through a longer club, you compromise accuracy. This is why the tour players, as a group, are not hitting fifty-inch drivers. As well as they swing a golf club, they are still not willing to give up accuracy. This should be taken as a caution by those of you who are going longer and longer but are not giving enough value to the importance of keeping your ball in play. One exception to consider would be for players who swing too fast or who have lost flexibility and, therefore, have an insufficient length in backswing. In this case, a longer club will help them feel the slower, longer swing they need. It can also help flatten out a swing that is too steep, even if used only for feel in practice.

Another vital element to consider is the overall weight of a club. Again, the modern technology of shaft and head materials has allowed club makers to take weight from the shaft, put it in the head, and increase the size of the head, while keeping the overall weight of the club lower than it was. So, I ask this question, How light is too light? Can you even get clubs too light? The answer to the latter question is definitely yes. Nearly twenty years ago a superlight club hit the golf market. Technically speaking, it made sense—yet the results were disastrous. There was a significant loss for the feel of the clubhead and the swing. Also, because of the sensation of being able to hit the ball farther, golfers began swinging these clubs faster and faster, throwing off tempo, pace, and ultimately sequence of motion. Their mishits felt terrible because of the lack of mass behind the hit.

Conversely, I did some tests with exceptionally heavy clubs and noted very interesting results with certain types of swings. Slicers, for example, whose natural downswing was out and over-the-top, came down on the inside with a heavier club. You can feel exactly the same thing if you swing a heavy training club. From the top, the heavy club simply makes the club fall into the slot rather than move into a position that creates an outside-in swing path. Obviously, there is a happy and correct medium for every player. It has to do with swing type, feel, swing speed, and preference.

A brief note on head design: If you are an outstanding ball striker, with a consistently good impact position, you may not need big perimeter-weighted clubheads. But for the average golfer, such clubheads can be very helpful. This means that what may be good for you won't necessarily be the same thing the tour player uses. Another clubhead feature that is similar in nature is an off-set model. Most professional players do not like the off-set feature in their irons because it promotes hooking, something they already may do, occasionally to excess. The average player who slices, however, would benefit greatly by such a feature. Slicers also need to pay attention to the elements of driver loft and it's face angle. The more loft built into the face, the less side spin will be imparted to the ball. A hook face will also minimize one's tendencies to hit the ball left to right. This is why the slicer often finds he or she can hit a 3 wood rather well even though the driver is difficult to control.

As technology has progressed, manufacturers have adapted wonderfully to golfers' weaknesses (and whims). Slicers (who make up approximately 80 percent of all players) have benefited the most. What I have found is that most slicers have a tendency to pull short irons and slice the longer clubs. Companies have reacted to this by making middle and long irons more upright and have also delofted all irons to allow these players to hit the ball straighter and farther with any given club. The more upright lie causes the sole of the club to rest unevenly on the ground, so that the toe is well off the turf. This causes the face to be more closed at impact, partially negating slice tendencies. Relative to its older counterpart, delofting an iron gives the golfer the impression he or she is hitting a certain club farther. Even though the face is more closed with less loft, the technological advancement of perimeter weighting still allows the golfer to get proper height to the shot.

In concluding this section, let me make it clear that all players should seek good fundamentals along with improving their sensitivity for the golf club. Your swing characteristics should be accommodated by clubs that fit. I am all for making the game easier by having technology assist your aspirations to be a better player. Also, it's nice to get excited about new clubs. After all, they can induce heightened confidence. Realize, however, that the golf club is only *part* of the game's grand, complex equation.

Instruction

In all the information I see that deals with helping people improve their golf swings, assistance in the area of selecting a teacher and taking lessons is almost nonexistent. A person can extract only so much from a tape, a magazine article, or television. There is no substitute for having a trained pair of eyes watch you hit a golf ball, a trained mind listen to the information you have previously absorbed, and a trained instructor give you realistic, objective feedback.

As I mentioned earlier, I strongly feel no beginner—child or adult—should take up the game without professional instruction. Clinics are fine at this stage and affordable to most. However, as you progress, there comes a time when you will need more individual attention on some kind of regular basis.

I advise the golfer, no matter how low his or her handicap, to take a lesson or two in the early spring to make sure everything is in place. I also recommend follow-up lessons throughout the season to ensure that no bad habits are creeping into the swing. These lessons may be scheduled only once a month or so, but they are extremely important.

At the beginning of every year, during his amateur days, and while

There's no substitute for having a pro with a trained pair of eyes watch you hit golf balls and then analyze your swing.

he played the PGA Tour full-time, Jack Nicklaus would have his teacher, Jack Grout, watch him hit balls and make sure everything was in place. Nicklaus's primary concern was on fundamentals: alignment, ball position, grip, etc. You might think that golf's greatest player wouldn't have to do this. Not so. No matter what level of player you are, it's extraordinarily easy for certain things to begin to be done incorrectly, unbeknown to the player himself or herself. This actually happens quite often with tour players.

Once I worked with PGA Tour player and former U.S. Open champion Lee Janzen and then didn't see him for about a month. When I left him his setup was perfect, and he was swinging great. Four weeks later, I saw him again. He was aligned yards right of target, but didn't know it. This fault was the source of his swing problem. The fact that things can go wrong so easily for tour players simply shows how easily they can go wrong for all of us. To nip this in the bud, we all need a periodic checkup; the longer your swing goes without a correction, the harder it will be to fix.

If you are already taking lessons from a professional instructor, I commend you. If not, I strongly urge you to seek out an instructor to assist you. Those of you who are club members have a head pro or teaching pro who is there to enhance your enjoyment of the game. Take advantage of that. Those of you who are not club members may not know that many teaching professionals at private clubs do take on a certain number of outside lessons. Many public, resort, and driving range facilities also employ qualified PGA-LPGA instructors.

If you are not currently taking lessons and would like to, I suggest taking the following steps. First, seek out an instructor who is a PGA or LPGA member. Preferably, this person is a full-time instructor who is very committed to helping students improve. I specify a PGA or LPGA member because these individuals are the best trained and most qualified. I recommend a full-time instructor because, simply, if one is totally focused on one endeavor, he or she is going to be better at it. Such an individual is going to think more intently and intelligently about the teaching process and generally be more conscientious. Recognizing that experience is the best teacher, I would find a full-time instructor who has at least three or four years under his or her belt, at a minimum. Another important area to consider is whether or not the instructor uses video. I would hope so; you need to see what you do. It also helps the instructor see things that cannot be seen during live action, and it helps you better understand what is wrong and better visualize what is right.

If you're thinking about a certain instructor, go in and have a talk. Get a sense of his or her communication skills, personality, and concern for students; all of these factors affect how you'll likely respond to the lessons. I would also like to know how to contact some of his or her current or former students, so that I might be able to chat with them about their lesson-taking experiences.

If you are not a member of a club but you would like to work with an instructor at one, I recommend you call and ask if he or she would be able to help you. If not, ask for recommendations of other teachers. Another approach is to call your local PGA office and ask for the names of teachers in your immediate area. The PGA of America is divided into forty-one geographical regions. Each section has an office headquarters with a full-time staff. People there will be happy to assist you with names and phone numbers. To find out the PGA Section and phone number for your area, call the PGA of America headquarters in Palm Beach Gardens, Florida.

Golf schools are another consideration. For the most part, nationally known schools are excellent. Some are better than others, but to a large degree how good a school is depends on where you are with your swing and what you want. I prefer small student to instructor ratios—no more than two to one. I feel most instructional situations require more individual attention than less. A higher ratio, however, is less expensive and thus more attractive to some golfers. I recommend that at your school of choice the ratio should not be higher than four to one, all else being considered.

It is a fallacy that because an instructor knows how to play golf exceptionally well, he or she automatically knows how to teach. What's vitally important is that the instructor have a good eye and know how to communicate the critical elements of the golf swing in a way that is meaningful for each student. When the lesson is over, you should want to practice and look forward to the next session. The teacher's fee should be commensurate with his or her ability and experience and be both fair and worthwhile.

Without question, the most revered attribute of a student is attitude. No matter what mechanical or physical problems arise, if the student has a good attitude there is no doubt in the instructor's mind that problems can be overcome. Two characteristics of a good attitude include a positive outlook and a receptiveness to the information being given that indicates trust. The student believes that there will be nothing to prevent improvement. This feeling must continue for the duration, despite inevitable minor setbacks. There is nothing more disconcerting to a teacher than to have a student whose enthusiasm is superficial and fleeting. Usually there are two reasons for this.

First, a student tends to pay too much attention to the golf ball and what it's doing at certain stages of a lesson. Of course, we all want the golf ball to be hit more solidly and accurately, but it's unrealistic to think that will always happen right away. Initially, the student may begin to make wonderful changes to the setup and/or swing, yet mishit the golf ball or even totally miss it. Some students immediately equate this with failure, lack of progress, or inability, which is totally incorrect. The ball may be slightly out of position for the new swing, or some other very minor problem may surface temporarily. The student becomes negative or frustrated, and all positive momentum is lost. The instructor wants the student simply to continue with the improved swing, to repeat the more correct motion so it can be instilled more deeply into the body. He knows the ball will soon just get in the way if the student doesn't concern himself with it.

The other aspect of this is the student's sense of reality coming into the lesson. Many students do not have an understanding of the process and think improvement will come much easier and/or faster than it usually does. When progress is slow, I make sure my own students understand this is normal and is nobody's fault. It's simply golf, plus the irrefutable fact that the body resists change. It will give in, but usually only gradually. The student must understand that just because the mind may know what to do, does not mean the body will be able to execute right away. The teacher can tell you, show you, and give you drills to improve your swing, but you must accept some degree of responsibility for training your body how to do this. I have no doubt that intellectually most students know this. Once involved in the process, however, many seem to lose sight of this fact of golfing life and become uneasy with the discomfort of change and with the fact that progress is gradual.

How long does this process of change take? It is different for everyone, so there is no specific answer. There are different levels of determination and desire, and everyone has a different availability for practice time. Different bodies learn and respond at different rates. There are variations in levels of athleticism, coordination, strength, flexibility, and motor skill. Realistic acknowledgment and acceptance of this, plus a willingness to do some degree of training as prescribed by the instructor, is all-important.

A good student is a good listener and asks questions rather than being an excessive talker who attempts to convey a certain knowledge of the swing. The good student is also receptive to new ideas and has a willingness to try changes to the setup and swing even if it's initially uncomfortable. In fact, the best students are the ones who can exaggerate movements the most and who are willing to feel the most uncomfortable (temporarily). If the student doesn't feel these sensations, no appreciable change is being made. Good students are not only willing to proceed this way but accept it as an integral part of improvement—ideally with a smile.

I've certainly covered a tremendous amount of territory in this opening chapter. I hope you agree, it was worth it. Now that you understand the building blocks for improving, you are well on your way to making the dream of better ball striking a reality.

The next steps involve learning exactly what makes good technique. The lessons that follow enable you to develop a swing that works for *you*, repeats itself under pressure, and produces powerfully accurate shots.

CHAPTER 2

The Golf Swing's Most Important Position

B efore turning this page, think for a moment about the answer to this question:

What is the most important position in the golf swing?

IMPACT!

Clockwise from top left: Ernie Els, Davis Love III, Annika Sorenstam, and Raymond Floyd.

Impact: dead square, dead solid perfect!

Impact—the moment of truth when club meets ball. No matter what your thoughts, what your intentions, whether you swing back fast or slow, long or short, upright or flat, the *only* thing the golf ball responds to is what the clubhead is doing at this moment.

It is of great interest to me that when I ask students the question I have just asked you, very rarely do I get *impact* for an answer. The responses commonly are setup, takeaway, top of backswing, or follow-through. It is possible to make an argument for these other positions; but if you are inclined to think this way, I ask you this: Is it absolutely impossible to strike a golf ball well if one of these other positions is incorrect? I think you would have to agree with me, the answer is *no*. However, if the impact position is incorrect and thus also contact between club and ball, it indeed is impossible. After all, when you really think about it, isn't everything we do before striking the ball expressly for the purpose of encouraging a correct meeting of the club with it? These other positions are a means to an end, the end itself being impact. This is the objective of it all.

The following relevant quote is from Jack Nicklaus:

I'm not a believer in methods. I'm a believer in fundamentals. Whatever any golfer does with a golf club should have only one purpose: to produce correct impact of club on ball. If he can achieve that consistently, the manner in which he does so doesn't really matter at all.

Bobby Jones, who I feel was one of golf's most insightful students of the swing, said:

The only reason we bother with form and the correct swing is to find the best way of consistently bringing about the proper set of conditions at impact. It helps a great deal, both to the understanding of the correct swing and the accomplishment of it, to have a clear picture of what ought to be happening at this instant.

As you can see, both Nicklaus and Jones recognized you should first have an understanding of what the club should be doing at impact before you become overly concerned with what you are doing before getting there.

One thing is certain, the impact position (left) *is not the same as the address position* (right).

What then is the correct impact position? Often I will ask a student to demonstrate for me what the positions of the body, arms, and club should be. Rarely does a student do this correctly. Most feel the impact position is similar to the address position, which is not at all the case. Golfers are so preoccupied with extraneous thoughts, they have lost sight of, misperceived, or never considered the one most important position of the swing—the position that should come before all others—impact!

In my opinion, if you do not understand what impact is or have not considered it, I don't know how can you possibly expect to arrive in this position correctly with any degree of regularity, if at all. As we have seen, you cannot afford to simply rely on a good setup and backswing. They certainly help encourage a good impact position, but they by no means guarantee it.

Let's now look at photographs showing two top professionals at

John Daly (left) *and Greg Norman* (right) *at impact. Note the similarities of this most vital of swing positions.*

impact: John Daly, who has a very unorthodox swing, and Greg Norman, whose technique is considered classic. View these photos carefully. See the similarity of the position of these major championship winners? If I were to show you the impact position of a hundred good ball strikers, you would see these common traits: body weight predominantly on the forward leg, right heel slightly elevated, both arms extended (with elbows close together and pointing downward, toward each hip), the back of the left wrist straight and in line with the forearm, both hands slightly in front of (or even with) the clubhead. Also, the hips are open approximately 30 degrees, and the shoulders are square or just slightly open. We know, too, that as similar as these players all look, their golf swings before impact are not the same. If you don't believe me, look at the backswing positions of Daly and Norman.

John Daly (left) *and Greg Norman* (right) *at the top of the backswing. Note the differences in their body and club positions.*

What we cannot see, but can presume, is that these observable features of the impact position equate to certain dynamics relative to the clubhead's movement. At the precise moment of impact, the clubhead is traveling along the target line, not going left or right. The clubface is square to the target, not open or closed. The clubhead is moving at optimum attainable speed. The ball is being struck in the center of the clubface, not toward the heel or toe, not toward its top or bottom. Finally, the clubhead has approached the ball from the proper angle of descent, not too steep or shallow.

From a physics standpoint, these are the only factors that determine how the ball will travel. We have to assume that they are all correct for Daly and Norman, and other powerfully accurate players, or these golfers would not be hitting great shots. These elements are referred to as the *ball flight laws* and are the only variables a golf ball responds to. These laws control a golf ball's response in every golf shot, from a three-foot putt to a three-hundred-yard drive. It seems logical to me that there would be a correlation between the impact position in which we consistently see so many great ball strikers and the success with which they correctly apply the laws of impact to the ball. These laws are what Jones and Nicklaus were referring to when they emphasized the importance of "bringing about the proper set of conditions at impact."

Going a step farther, if I were to prioritize these five laws, I would put them in the following order of importance:

1. Clubhead path
2. Clubface position relative to the path
3. Angle of club's approach to ball
4. Solid contact
5. Clubhead speed

This order would be for all levels of golfers, assuming they have reached the point of being able to consistently make contact with the ball.

The definition of *clubhead path* is somewhat arbitrary, but I would define it as the direction of movement of the clubhead over a distance of thirty-six inches in the hitting area—eighteen inches on either side of the golf ball.

My reasoning for placing more importance on path than on clubface

Correct path movement has the clubhead moving to the ball slightly from inside the target line (left), *then right along it at impact and just after* (right).

position is that the path is related strongly to the plane. Furthermore, the plane has a very strong influence on the position of the clubface during the downswing and, ultimately, at impact. Yes, I agree, the grip is another influencing factor, but whatever the grip position, a steep downswing plane strongly encourages an open clubface at impact. A shallow plane promotes a closed face position. This is a dynamic of the golf swing that I feel does not receive sufficient attention.

For example, a person who has a strong grip will still predominantly slice the ball with an outside-in swing path, with his longer clubs, rather than hit a pull-hook. This is because the steepness of the downswing plane causes the forearms, hands, and wrists to counter-rotate in such a manner that the clubface opens at impact, which, by rights, should be closed owing to the grip. Specifically, the steep downswing plane causes the left arm to buckle and the left wrist to break down. Again, the effect is to open the clubface rather than have it rotate correctly, which occurs when the left arm remains straight and the back of the left wrist remains flat.

Conversely, if the player's downswing plane becomes too horizontally oriented or flat, and he or she swings on too much of an inside-out path, the clubface responds by closing excessively—even if the player's grip is weak. This is why many low handicap players fight hooks; and after hooking shot after shot, they try to manipulate the clubface into an open position by an incorrect use of their hands and wrists at impact, aiming farther right or by changing their body action. In short, they fail to address their true problem.

The slicer does a similar thing but in the opposite manner. He or she will tend to aim more left, move the ball too far forward in the stance, and then try to manipulate the clubface into a closed position. When such a player slices badly he or she feels handcuffed at impact, often saying, "I cannot get the club through the ball." The slicer will also falsely sense that the harder he or she swings down, the better the chance he or she will have in preventing the ball from going right. Ironically, the opposite is true. The more aggressive the downswing, the worse the slice pattern.

I certainly understand the argument that some teachers make for other laws such as the clubface position at impact being the number-one priority of the swing. Some say that if an outside-in swinger could manage to close his or her heretofore open clubface, the ball would fly left rather than slice. This in turn would induce the golfer to approach the ball on a path that is more from the inside. The problem I have with this approach is that such golfers are trying to close the clubface while swinging on a plane that is trying to open it. Moreover, even if the golfers do succeed occasionally in closing the clubface and hit a few shots left of target, as much as they may then desire to swing down more from the inside, they still will be fighting all their natural tendencies to swing on an outside-in path. In this instance I've found such players instinctively take the easy way out by simply aiming too far to the right to compensate for a ball that is going left.

I prefer to attack the path problem first along with the grip, if necessary. I want the student to learn the correct impact position of the body with the clubhead approaching the ball well from the inside. Success here usually results in pushes or push-fades initially, because even though the new inside path encourages a better rotation or closing of the clubface, the imprint of the wrong wrist, hand, and forearm motion is so strong it tends to temporarily override the correcting influence of the path. In such a case, I have the student perform drills that promote the correct rotation of the clubface, but never at the expense of losing the inside path. Once the clubface starts closing, the golfer can soon let go of any conscious effort to make this happen.

What about the other three impact laws: angle of approach, solid contact, and clubhead speed? I have positioned them third, fourth, and fifth because they, too, are strongly influenced by clubhead path and clubface position.

In regard to speed, many golfers need to improve their accuracy, not just distance. This is why I believe clubhead path and clubface position come first. The better the path, usually the better the plane. The better the plane, the more powerful the hit. More clubhead speed will be gen-

You want the clubhead to approach the ball from inside the target line. The more correct the plane, and thus usually the path, the more solid the impact.

erated because, among other things, centrifugal force comes into play in a correct swing, helping any golfer create more power than he or she otherwise could. So by improving path (a directional component), you increase clubhead speed. Furthermore, the more correct the path, and thus usually the plane, the more solid the contact. Solid contact is another distance-enhancing feature.

Clubface position also plays a key role in producing solid contact. If the clubface is open or shut to the path, the heel or toe will usually contact the ball first. If the clubface is square, the ball will be more apt to be hit on the sweetspot. This is another example of a directional component (clubface position) enhancing distance—in this case through solid contact.

Angle of approach can be thought of as synonymous with the plane of the downswing. It, too, has a strong relationship with the path of the clubhead. In fact, path and angle of approach are so interconnected that either

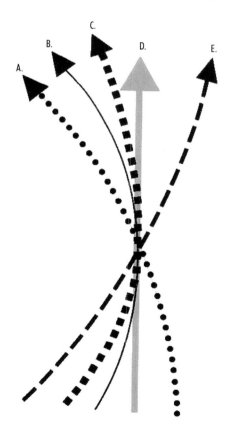

A. Outside-in (severe)
B. Still outside-in (less severe)
C. Correct path (inside-ALONG-inside)
D. Target line
E. Inside-out

Studying this drawing will help you appreciate some important elements of the swing, most notably the path of the clubhead through the impact area.

could be first in my prioritized list of the laws governing impact. To understand this relationship better and also have a clearer understanding of the correct path itself, look at the drawing on the previous page.

As the clubhead moves down on its correctly prescribed arc, it approaches the target line—and golf ball—from the inside. However, since the arc is tangent to the straight target line, the clubhead swings along that line at impact, then returns to the inside as it ascends in the through-swing. This movement is commonly referred to as *inside-along the target line-inside.*

I have noted the incorrect paths of a club approaching too much from the inside as well as too much from the outside. In regard to the latter, I think it is of interest to note that an outside-in downswing path does not necessarily mean the club swings outside the target line before impact and then across it as it contacts the ball. This is the usual explanation of outside-in, and indeed this motion can and does occur; however, it is an extreme example of outside-in. The worst of shots results. As the drawing shows, an incorrect downswing approach could have the clubhead outside the proper arc, yet still inside the target line. It is still outside-in, except outside is with reference to the correct arc, or plane, not the target line. Pulls, slices, and weak heeled shots are still the result.

The relationship of angle of approach to path is that the steeper the approach, usually the more outside-in the path. Conversely, the more shallow the angle of approach, usually the more inside-out the path. Thankfully, when the angle of approach is just right, the path is usually also correct: from inside, to along the target line, back to the inside. The opposite is also true. If your swing path with the clubhead is correct, your angle of approach will be just fine.

I recognize that all the ball flight laws are important and are closely interrelated. But by focusing on path first, then clubface, the other three laws usually fall nicely into place. If any particular student needs a different order to make faster progress, that can easily be done. However, juggling the order of priority would involve only path, clubface, and angle of approach. I would let centeredness and speed respond as indirect beneficiaries of the improvement of the others.

Not only should you have a clear understanding of the impact position and what the club should be doing at this moment but also you should know what is happening from a dynamic, motion standpoint; in other words, know what the correct impact position should accomplish in the early postimpact positions. Here, I am primarily focusing on the movement of the arms, hands, wrists, and club.

On occasion, students swing into what appears on video to be an acceptable impact position, yet the shot is poor, indicating it really wasn't. Usually a poor impact is easily seen, so this example is fairly rare. However, it serves to make a point. The postimpact positions of the student reveal why the shot was hit poorly. For example, a major breakdown of the left wrist and arm will suddenly appear. In such instances, even though the impact position may appear to be good, in the dynamic sense it wasn't. The right hand, for example, was just at this moment

Simulated Impact Drill

Step 1: simulate the impact position.

Step 2: make a very short backswing, primarily hinging the wrists but also employing a short arm swing. The body maintains its starting position.

Step 3: with a continuous motion, swing the club down and through the ball to the finish position shown here. Your thought here is to extend the arms and rotate the clubshaft and clubface.

becoming excessively forceful and overactive, the golfer attempting to "release" the club or rotate the clubface into a closed position. Why would he or she be doing this? Maybe the golfer had an extremely open clubface owing to an incorrect grip. Or maybe he or she had an incorrect perception of release. Does this sound familiar?

A drill I use quite often for problems in this area is the *Simulated Impact Drill.* (See previous page and above.) I have the student set up to a golf ball with a 7 or 8 iron; then I have him or her simply simulate the correct impact position. Next, I have the student make a very short on-plane backswing motion, primarily by hinging the wrists, but accompanied also by a slight arm swing. All the while the body remains in the impact position. With continuous motion, the club is swung smoothly back to the ball—not forcefully. The shot flies only fifteen or twenty yards. I also have the student hold and analyze the finish position, which is relatively short. By doing this, the student gains a sense of where everything should be at impact and how a ball should be struck when on the ground. By monitoring the postimpact position, the student also feels and understands what is happening from a dynamic, continuous motion sense, (as the club and body move correctly through impact to the proper position beyond).

Let's now move on to earlier positions of the golf swing and see what might be the optimum way for a golfer to successfully arrive into the impact position.

CHAPTER 3

The Backswing

Remember the photographs of John Daly and Greg Norman in Chapter 2? To further prove that everyone need not do the same thing in the backswing to arrive in a good impact position and hit good golf shots, take a look at these photographs of Fred Couples and Lee Janzen. Although their backswing actions vary, they look like twins at impact.

What is of paramount importance is *if* impact of club to ball is correct, relative to the dynamics of clubhead motion (laws), it really doesn't matter what took place beforehand. In fact, even if your backswing is technically wrong, you will still be able to hit good shots *if* your impact is correct. That is the good news.

The bad news is, as we saw earlier with our hypothetical group of one hundred students, even if you make a technically perfect backswing, there is no guarantee you will hit a good shot. It all comes back to your ability to achieve a technically correct impact position, meaning that the dynamics of the club's motion and the body's position are correct at this

John Daly

Fred Couples

Notice the major differences in the takeaways of these great players. Though different here, all three look alike as they start down, and are practically identical at impact.

Lee Janzen

moment. These two elements are basically synonymous. In short, you can't have one with any degree of consistency without the other.

Some additional bad news is that what I said earlier about being able to hit good shots even with a technically incorrect backswing does not give you license to do whatever you want. In regard to very unorthodox swingers, such as John Daly or Lee Trevino, there is a strong qualifier. Even though their backswings are unique, they are exceptional athletes with superior feel, training, and experience. They also have an acute sensitivity and awareness of where the club is during the swing.

It would be fair to say that when a good player—pro or amateur—swings the club back incorrectly, off-plane, it feels different from when it is on plane. Specifically, an off-plane club feels heavier in the backswing than one that is on plane. For good players, this heavy feel may help trigger the initiation of a corrective process that allows them to move the club into better positions during the course of the rest of the

Lee Trevino takes the club back well above the ideal plane (left), *but he still hits the ball very solidly and very accurately due to his ability to reroute the club through the rest of his swing and ultimately, achieve such a good position at impact* (right).

swing. Such players have the unique ability to swing the club initially in an unorthodox manner, but within the time of say one second, are able to reroute the club from its technically incorrect position to a conventionally perfect impact.

The average player who starts the club back incorrectly is not talented enough to make in-swing corrections. He or she doesn't have the same sensitivity and feel of where the club is to even know it may be out of position at a certain point in the backswing. That is why, with a similar backswing fault, the recreational player hits poor shots, while the tour player hits good ones. The incorrect takeaway, the incorrect backswing, the incorrect top-of-backswing position, all become part of a chain reaction that leads to a faulty downswing and, ultimately, to a poor impact. Misperceptions, inherent tendencies, and physical limitations all play a role here. The tour player has learned to break the natural chain reaction an incorrect backswing produces through practice, hard work, training, feel, and a correct understanding of where he or she is trying to get at impact. The average player, therefore, cannot always use the "mistake" of a tour player as justification for a similar flaw.

We must also recognize these tour players are the exception to the rule. For every professional player who has an incorrect backswing, there are perhaps one hundred who are technically perfect or who are at least trying to be. Why? Because even though there is no guarantee one good position breeds others, it tends to. In addition, the fewer compensations in the swing, the less chance for error—and the greater chance for consistency. Tour players know this.

If you want to correct an unsound takeaway/backswing move, the professional who makes exactly the opposite unorthodox move may be a good example and image on which to focus. In other words, once you have identified incorrect positions of your own takeaway and backswing, try to emulate the takeaway/backswing of a professional who makes a move in the opposite manner. This is an approach that takes you away from a mechanics mode and allows you to get more into a mimic mode, which is easier for most people. This also conveys a point I constantly use in my teaching: To make a correction, you must feel exaggeration in your efforts.

This is precisely what I did with Rocco Mediate when we restructured his golf swing in 1988. Rocco was taking the club back too much to the inside, and it was creating problems that he could not compensate for. It was not until I had Rocco simulate the backswing of Calvin Peete that he was able to make real progress in eliminating this mistake. Calvin's takeaway and backswing were exactly the opposite of what Rocco had been doing and provided an image Rocco could envision and immediately relate to.

For every Lee Trevino, Fred Couples, and Jim Furyk—for every John Daly, Ray Floyd, and Nancy Lopez—there are, as I previously mentioned, hundreds of professional players, such as Lee Janzen, who are technically correct or who are working on being so in the takeaway, in the backswing, and at the top. In other words, there is some degree of agreement about what is the most correct way to swing the club. Teachers and professional players generally agree, the better the takeaway, the better your chance of employing a good halfway-back position. The better your halfway-back position, the better your chance of being correct at the top. And if you are in a good at-the-top position, and get there correctly, the better your opportunity to return the club to a solid, square impact position. This is particularly true if you know what *the* impact position is and work faithfully on a drill that can teach you how to get there. The Simulated Impact Drill (Chapter 2) is such a drill.

Although there are exceptions to the rules, the better your backswing positions (this page *and* facing page), *the better your opportunity to return the club to a square, solid impact position.*

One of the real talents of a good teacher, then, is expressed in his or her ability to know when to change an incorrect move and when not to. Frankly, one of the most difficult things in teaching average players is that most require change because they are unable to make compensations for early errors the way a professional can. When I can get away with not making a change, I will. It reflects the fact that some mistakes are far better than others. But if changes have to be made, we run headlong into all the obstacles discussed in Chapter 1. Even so, it usually is the best way to improve one's golf swing.

This reminds me of an often occurring situation when a student comes to me for a session and complains that he or she just had a lesson from someone else and that teacher tried to "change everything." I get the impression that some students want to acquire a better swing but at the same time don't want to change anything, or change very little. These are usually the people who have the most things wrong with their swing.

When I question such students about all the changes they were directed to make, they often relate only a few. I explain to them that if they're hitting the ball poorly or inconsistently, and they want a lesson to improve their swing, some change must occur in the process. It's simply an appeal to logic, with the hope that logic will override human nature, which always seems to have us want things to come easy. On the other hand, occasionally students *can* be given too much advice at one time, overloading their systems, which is a situation teachers have to be careful of and avoid at all costs. But, if you are to improve a deficient swing, some change is unavoidable.

Look at this average player in the most common bad-impact position. Note the difference between his hitting position and those of the pros previously shown or those that appear in the color insert.

What do you see? Notice the weight has not shifted well to the front leg. The right heel is still grounded. The arms are certainly not straight, separating the elbows well away from one another with the left elbow facing more upward and outward, rather than downward toward the left hip. Notice also the back of the left hand is not straight, in line with the forearm, and the hands are more behind the clubhead. The shoulder line is open, rather than square, and the hips are excessively open; sometimes as much as 70 or 80 degrees, rather than 25 or 30 degrees.

How do you suppose these positions relate to the dynamic movement of the clubhead? The clubhead path most often is swinging too abruptly to the left. The clubhead is approaching the ball from too steep an angle. The clubface is too open (usually) or too closed. The ball is not contacted in the center of the clubface, and clubhead speed is not what it could be. All the impact laws have been compromised. If you are an average player who tends to slice or pull the golf ball, I have just described what your clubhead is doing at impact, and you can bet your impact position looks similar to those of the people pictured.

As Bobby Jones said, we are trying to find the best way of "consistently bringing about the proper set of conditions at impact." And, as I said earlier, there is some agreement about what is best.

So what is the best way? It's whatever works consistently. For most players, this is a movement that can be described as fundamentally sound, in agreement with geometric principles and laws of motion.

Let's look at what ideal movement entails and at some of the most common deviations of average players that result in poor impact positions, including, but not limited to, the one just described.

I will discuss the fundamentals of the setup in Chapter 6, but for now, assume the correct in-swing positions I am about to describe begin from a sound setup. Notice my starting position in the photographs below to get a sense of correct posture, body lines (alignment), and position of club and ball.

The beginning of the backswing is commonly referred to as the *takeaway*. Specifically, it deals with the first thirty-six to forty-two inches of the clubhead's movement and the first twelve inches or so of the hands and arms.

Of all the students I work with, I would say no more than two or three in a hundred execute this move correctly. Most suffer the consequences at impact. They never recover, and a chain reaction is set off that they are unable to compensate for. As we discussed, a compensation is not impossible, but it takes extraordinary talent to consistently execute.

One of the problems of the takeaway is that golfers become too fixated on the movement of one end of the club and don't respect the

The basic setup position for the driver. The spine is straight but tilted, knees slightly flexed, chin is up, rear end back and out.

movement of the other. As golfers get entangled with questions about the movement of the clubhead (straight back? inside?) and the clubface (what exactly is square?), they totally ignore proper movement of the club's butt end.

Look at the photographs below of a correct takeaway. First, the movement is initiated by the arms. There can be a slight, concurrent movement of the body laterally to the right, but there doesn't have to be. The primary emphasis of motion is in the arms. There should be no attempt to do anything with the hands or wrists. There should be no conscious effort to turn anything—not the shoulders, hips, forearms, or clubface. The shoulders will begin to move, but only in response to the movement of the arms.

As the arms start the club back, the clubhead is moving gradually upward and inward. It is a proper blend of the in-and-up movement that has the clubhead on plane. But for this to happen, the butt end of the club must be moving in precisely the same manner as the clubhead, only on a smaller scale. The butt end should also move on an inward and upward arc—it is also "on plane." This can be seen in the following two drawings.

The correct takeaway action from the face-on view (left) *and from the down-target line view* (right).

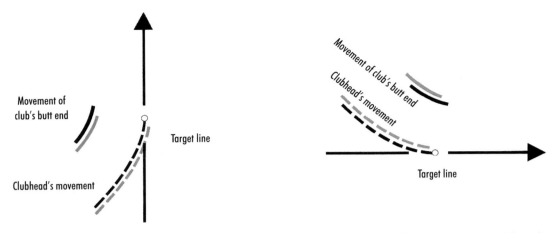

The upward and inward movement of the club's head and butt end, shown here from the down-target line view (left) *and the face-on view* (right).

If we draw an imaginary line along the golfer's clubshaft at address, we establish what is called the *shaft angle plane*. If the takeaway is initiated correctly, both ends of the club move back and up along this diagonal plane line.

Most golfers who make an improper takeaway move the butt end of the club outward, above the shaft angle plane. When this occurs, the clubhead can move outward also or it can move excessively inward, under the shaft angle plane. In either case, the club is now in an incorrect, off-plane position. When the butt end and clubhead are above—outside the plane—the takeaway is similar to Fred Couples's (shown earlier), Lee Trevino's, and Jim Furyk's. When the butt end is above the plane, but the clubhead has moved under it, the takeaway is similar to Nancy Lopez's.

To hit good shots if the former occurs or if the butt end is on plane with just the clubhead above it, you must reroute the club inward, back onto plane, sometime during the rest of the backswing or in the downswing. Failing that, the downswing plane will be too outside-above. The latter scenario is much more common: butt end out, clubhead under. A slight variation has the clubhead moving too inside, under the plane with the butt end staying on the plane. In either case, the clubhead and clubshaft are well out of position. There has been too much "in" movement of the clubhead without the proper blend of up. The consequences are interesting. Either the golfer keeps the club in this under-the-plane position as it returns to the ball or, during the completion of the backswing, he or she experiences a severe lifting as a natural reaction to the excessive flatness earlier.

When Floyd does this, he begins a corrective process that puts the club beautifully on plane as he starts down. When the average player lifts, it is excessive. This creates a chain reaction that throws the clubhead outward and over the plane in the downswing. The result is a cut-across outside-in swing path at impact, usually with the clubface very open, particularly with the longer clubs. I refer to this move as *in, up, and over.* (See next page.)

The golfer who doesn't lift the club but keeps it on the flat inside path back approaches the ball on an exaggerated inside-out swing path. As a result, he or she tends to hit pushes or hooks, as well as fat and thin shots.

Why do these faults occur? The reasons are many and varied, but usually it gets back to things we discussed earlier. For example, a poor grip (inherent tendency) causes the clubface to fan open immediately in the takeaway. A clubface that is fanning open invariably causes the clubhead to move back too far inside, under the plane. Another possible scenario is that the golfer simply has a misperception of how the clubhead should be moving in the initial stages.

This is precisely why old adages, such as Take the club back low and inside, can be so damaging. It also explains why, when asked a particular question by a student, I always say, "There are two answers." First is the answer of what is technically correct. Second is the answer that relates to what this particular student should be feeling relative to his or her own individual problems of which I'm aware.

For example, say a student—who takes the clubhead too inside, under the plane—asks me if the clubhead should come straight back. My answer would be no, technically it doesn't. But because she takes it excessively inside, I would tell her she should *feel* it come straight back. In fact, she might have to consciously try to cock her wrists early and pick the club up, before we see the clubhead coming back anywhere close to the proper plane.

A person's takeaway could be faulty because of an improper setup, as well. Another cause of the incorrect takeaway could simply be owing to one's misperception of the plane of the golf swing. I have never had a student indicate to me that he or she thought the golf swing plane was perfectly horizontal, but I have had many tell me they thought it was perfectly vertical. For discussion's sake, let's just say the swing plane is a

The in (above, left), *up* (above, right), *and over* (left) *movements.*

tilted circle, or ellipse. The tilt is inward, toward the golfer, putting the plane on a diagonal. If your perception is that it is a Ferris wheel (vertical), I'm sure you can see how the clubhead would be lifted above the correct plane immediately in the takeaway.

The point, however, is that whatever is causing the incorrect motion should be sought out and identified. I don't like to just treat the symptom by telling the student what to do. I want to also identify the root cause of the mistake, and often this requires getting into the student's head. Trying to fix a takeaway without proceeding this way is wasted effort. Otherwise, there will always be conflict in the student's mind.

Let's now move on to the next stage of the backswing which I refer to as *Position 1*. The shaft of the club is parallel to the ground. To help you appreciate this vital swing position, it is shown here from two different angles. One photograph shows me swinging a driver; the other, a 5 iron.

Notice that the clubshaft is below waist level and parallel to the target line. The butt end of the club is only two to three inches to the right of

Here I am, in Position 1, with the driver (left). *Here I am, in my practice station, grooving Position 1 with a 5 iron* (right).

the right foot, while the shaft is opposite the ball of the right foot. The clubface is parallel to my spine angle, not in a toe-up position, as is commonly believed. The right arm is visible above the left. My weight is already into the right leg, which remains flexed slightly at the knee. The shoulders have begun to turn, but only about 30 degrees of the full 90 degrees desired and only owing to the movement of the arms, not to any conscious effort. The wrists are beginning to hinge, but only because of the movement and weight of the clubhead.

The next position of the backswing, referred to as *Position 2*, is an in-between position, between Position 1 and the top of the backswing, which will be identified as *Position 3*.

In Position 2, the left arm is approximately parallel to the ground. Because the wrists have been hinging dynamically as I pass through Position 1 and because the arms are swinging up on the right plane, the clubshaft now is seen above the original shaft angle plane. If the shaft is still on it's original shaft angle plane, or worse yet under it, the club is dangerously out of position. In regard to the shaft's position above it, it

Here I am, in Position 2 of the backswing, swinging a 5 iron.

is interesting to note we have leeway for variation here. The clubshaft can be anywhere within a zone that begins at parallel and above the original shaft angle plane to an angle of about 76 degrees to the vertical, depending on the club being swung. Any more vertical than that and you are moving the club too far off the plane, which is going to require a compensating move later. Ideally, I like to see the shaft here on an angle of about 55 to 56 degrees, again, depending on the club.

The wrists are fully hinged here. The left arm is extended, but not stiff. The right arm has folded, but with the elbow slightly away from the side. The back of the left wrist is straight and in line with the forearm. The body's weight has now moved well onto the right side (weight shift about 80 percent complete) with the right knee steady and flexed. The shoulders have now turned about 60 of the full 90 degrees, but ideally there has been no conscious effort to turn the hips or lift the left hee.

This presupposes that the golfer has good flexibility. If he or she doesn't, then closing the stance slightly, making a conscious effort to turn the hips, and/or allowing the left heel to come up to assist the effort are all acceptable compensations. The bottom line: Make whatever adjustments necessary to alter the motion at this point so that the club will be positioned as correctly as possible by the time it arrives at the top.

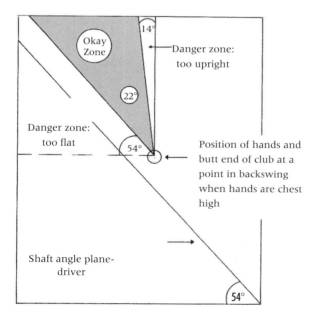

This drawing shows the okay *and* danger *zones, relative to the shaft angle plane, when swinging a driver.*

Let me now note the variation of the positions of the clubshaft, based on the faulty takeaways previously discussed. The comparisons are really quite simple. In the faulty positions, the shaft is either too flat or too upright compared to the correct position. The shaft can be only above plane or below it at any point during the swing, if it is not on it. Insofar as terminology is concerned, *flat, too horizontal, inside, under,* and *below* are synonymous. *Upright, too vertical, outside, over,* and *above* are synonymous for the opposite condition.

An incorrect swing isn't necessarily always on one plane (below) or the other (above) throughout its entirety. For example, in some swings, it's possible to be above (takeaway), below (Positions 1 and 2), above (Position 3, top), and below (Position 4). However, if you are not on it, you can be only above it or below it. In a fundamentally correct swing the shaft is on plane throughout its entire motion.

As we go from each successive position to the next, we are getting closer and closer to impact. Therefore, it becomes more and more important to be more and more correct as we move along. At the top—Position 3—we are only about one-half second from impact, so this position better be pretty good. You don't have a lot of time to fix it. And,

Here I am in Position 3, at the top of the backswing.

if it isn't good here, you'd better be well into your compensation process, or a good shot will not ensue.

Like Position 2, Position 3 allows for latitude, insofar as defining what correct is. Variations in expert players' positions here are primarily based on desired trajectory (high, medium, or low) and flight pattern (draw, straight, fade). Stature, arm length, flexibility, and strength can also be factors. Ben Hogan, for example, learned to play golf in the winds of Texas, which required a lower ball flight. He, therefore, gravitated toward a position that was flatter at the top. Initially, he also hooked the ball. Jack Nicklaus, on the other hand, learned to play at Ohio's Scioto Country Club, a course that had smallish greens and softer fairways. A higher, softer shot pattern was more ideally suited to that type of course, so Nicklaus developed an upright swing that produced soft-landing fades. Neither Hogan's at-the-top position or Nicklaus's is more correct, even though they are different. What is of even greater importance, however, is that each of their downswings and follow-throughs match their backswings and positions at the top. This is a topic I will discuss in more detail later.

Tiger Woods's top-of-backswing position is between that of Hogan and Nicklaus and is considered fundamentally correct. In fact, I consider it the *model* position. But, even though each of the three is slightly different in regard to the pitch of the left arm, there remain great similarities among them at this point in the swing.

1. The left wrist is virtually straight, in line with the forearm.
2. The clubface is square, angled downward, approximately parallel to the left arm and wrist.
3. The hands are above the height of the right shoulder, and the shoulders are on an angle consistent with the tilt of the upper body at address.
4. The left arm is straight, but not rigid.
5. The right arm is away from the side, the forearm is approximately parallel to the spine, and the upper arm is parallel to the ground.
6. The shaft is parallel to the target line (if it is swung back far enough to be parallel to the ground).

It's interesting to note here the symmetry that is usually seen in Position 1 and Position 3. If the club is too inside and angled back at Position

Tiger Woods, Jack Nicklaus, and Ben Hogan at the top. Note the different angle of the left arm in the swings of these great players.

1, usually it will be in the same basic position at the top—referred to as *across the line,* because the clubhead end of the shaft is pointing across the target line. It's possible to move the club up to what's referred to as a *laid-off position* at the top from an inside takeaway, but this is not as common. What is far more prevalent is the laid-off position resulting from a takeaway that is outside, above the plane. Again, you'll notice the symmetry of the shaft in these two positions.

In either case, the laid-off and across-the-line positions are not recommended, requiring a compensatory move down to put the shaft of the club back on plane. The across-the-line position usually results in pushes and/or hooks and fat and thin shots (too much of an inside downswing); but occasionally the over-the-top tendency can be strong enough to override the too-inside downswing and cause the golfer to move the club out and above the plane anyway.

This type of downswing is also the most common result of the laid-off shaft. The clubhead and shaft move out and above the correct plane, resulting in cuts and pulls. If this movement is exaggerated, shanks, tops, and thin, heeled shots occur.

In addition to the features of Position 3 noted earlier, there are some other important elements to consider. The right knee has remained flexed. The shoulders have turned approximately 90 degrees; but the hips, resisting, have turned much less. This is accomplished, ideally, with the left heel on the ground and with space between the knees. The upper body, as it has coiled, has moved over the inside of the right leg. The angle of the back has inclined away from the target, and the left shoulder and center of head are vertically over a point just inside the right knee. The relationship of the shaft, stance, and target lines are all parallel. Again, the clubface is square, which means it is on an angle that corresponds to the angle of the left arm—approximately 45 degrees.

From this position, the golfer has a wonderful opportunity to deliver a solid, accurate, and powerful blow to the golf ball. There is no guarantee this will happen, as we noted earlier. But at least the player hasn't put the club in a position that precludes any possibility of hitting a good shot or a position that requires compensations that he or she might not be able to make.

We are now ready to move down.

CHAPTER 4

The Downswing

I recognize there are some who say there really is no top of backswing, because when the club stops moving back in the expert's swing, it is the result of some part of the body having already started moving forward. I agree. Having said that, there is one final position wherein there is no longer backward movement of the arms and club, regardless of what causes this to happen. I referred to this position previously as *the top*. Dynamically speaking, this area of the swing is also referred to as *the transition,* which correctly has more of a connotation of motion. I say correctly because proper sequence of motion has the body moving first in the downswing, with the arms and club following close behind. This is an extremely critical area of the swing and an area in which I see major discrepancies between good and poor swingers.

The poor swinger, starting down, instinctively wants to do something first with the arms, hands, or upper right side or use some combination of all three. This would be the hit instinct kicking in. Remember our

On the downswing, the lower body leads, while the arms and club follow close behind.

example of the hypothetical one hundred students who learned perfect setups, backswings, and top-of-backswing positions? A large percentage, I surmised, would execute the downswing incorrectly, most outside-in, over the top. In other words, a perfect backswing only encourages a correct downswing—it doesn't guarantee it. It's possible to start down incorrectly from a perfect backswing and still hit poor shots. I gave you the one hundred students example to emphasize that golfers have incorrect downswing tendencies even before hitting their first shot. Now also consider the mistakes that can be made in the backswing, as we have discussed, that can cause a chain reaction that moves the club over the top as it swings down. When the ball is struck, usually with an open clubface, it goes to the right. Unfortunately, this induces the player to make the same incorrect move next time, only with greater intensity; the swing becomes even more outside-in (swing path left) to counter the ball that is going right. All these natural or developed tendencies result in a motion that is contrary to sound technique.

Before looking at the mechanics and positions of the downswing, I would like you to first establish in your mind the foundation of the move down that allows for correct positions of the club to occur. This relates to sequence of motion; and sequence of motion in the forward move in golf is no different from that of other basic athletic motions. The tennis player steps first (body), then swings (arms). The bowler steps first, then delivers the ball. The baseball pitcher winds up, steps forward, then throws. The batter lifts the forward leg (shifts weight back), steps forward into the pitch (shifts weight forward), then swings.

The golf swing is exactly the same, although we don't step. We simply move the hips in a manner that shifts the body weight forward, in balance. And this move forward of the lower left side, from hip to knee, actually begins as the club, arms, and shoulders are still moving back. It is precisely the correct execution of this movement, ideally together with a sound arm, club, and body motion in the backswing, that causes the hands, arms, and club to move down on the correct plane, rather than above or below it. You may be able to better see now that players who have even the best of mechanics can break those mechanics down if they succumb to the hit instinct and get quick with the hands and arms, disallowing the body to perform its required first move in the downswing.

Let's now look a little more closely at the precise movement of the hips in the downswing, because I think a lot of golfers misunderstand what they need to be doing here. How are the hips moving to transfer the body weight forward, while in balance? What about common adages we so often hear relative to this aspect of the swing? Turn the hips. Slide the hips. Or clear the hips. Are these good thoughts? I don't think so because they are ambiguous and misleading.

Just like the arc on which the butt end of the club travels, and just like the arc of the clubhead itself, the hips in the downswing also move on an arc. Therefore, in actuality, the hips do not just clear or turn; nor do they just slide. Rather, they do all three.

If the left hip is moving on an arc you could say it's sliding and turning at the same time; in other words, there is the correct blend of lateral and rotational movement. Specifically, the left hip moves more laterally first, which moves weight to the forward leg, then moves more rotationally as the body and arms move to impact and beyond. If you are a good

Look closely at the movement of the hips in all four photographs so that you form a clear visual image of the proper downswing action.

player, your tendency will be to put too much slide (lateral motion) in your movement, causing hooks, blocks, and pushes, which means clear or turn *may* be a correct thought for you *if* it helps you restore the proper amount of rotation.

On the other hand, if you slice or pull shots, your tendency will be to already turn or clear the left hip excessively. This often happens as a result of an outward arm, hand, and upper-right-side body motion when starting down. Or if, for whatever reason, you simply have a propensity to keep your weight back on your rear foot as you swing the club down, your left hip will clear or spin excessively, causing the arms, hands, and club to move out. It is the old chicken or the egg story, but whichever occurs first (for some it's one, for others it's the other) both are happening and both must be eliminated. In any event, there is too much turn (rotational motion) in your hip movement, which causes pulls, slices, tops, and thin shots. Thus clearing or turning your hips in the downswing is the worst thought you can have. You need more slide, more lateral action in your downswing.

That is why I so often cringe when listening to television golf commentators remarking on a player's hip-clearing action. This is not what the average player should be hearing. Most club-level golfers already

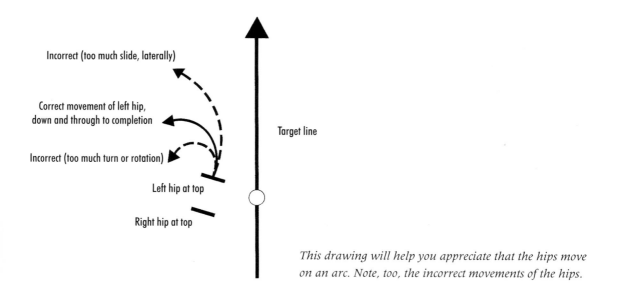

This drawing will help you appreciate that the hips move on an arc. Note, too, the incorrect movements of the hips.

exaggerate this downswing action. Besides, what professionals are working on or need to do in their swings often has no bearing on what the average player needs to do. Ideally, there would always be a disclaimer from the TV commentators: "If you slice, pull, or pull-hook, this hip action is not for you."

This also points out the fact that even though we can segregate and examine arm motion and body motion in the swing separately, there is a strong relationship between the two. The better your arms swing, the better your body motion tends to be. The better your body motion, the better your arm swing tends to be. Conversely, if you have poor body motion, your arm swing usually will also be poor. Or, if your arm swing is poor, bad body motion usually will be a consequence.

Now that we have established correct sequencing and how the lower body works, let's look back at Daly, Norman, Couples, and Janzen as they start the downswing. We saw earlier how they had dissimilarities in the backswing. But we also saw that by impact they all looked virtually identical, in the position both of their clubs and of their bodies. At what point then do they stop looking different and start looking more similar? Is it not until impact or is it sooner? In fact, it is sooner. It is here, as the initial move down is made. Their shaft and arm positions may not be identical, but they are very similar. They are all sequencing correctly and their bodies are in the same position. I call this position *Position 4*—one-third of the way down.

Look at the position of the shaft first. It is neither vertical nor horizontal. It is on a diagonal that is parallel and above the original angle of the shaft at address. The shaft is also between the arms, with the clubhead behind the body. (A line drawn vertically downward to the ground would not touch the golfer's body at any point.) Also note the angle between the left arm and club shaft: It is 90 degrees or less, indicating the wrists are not uncocking prematurely. The hips are now opening, but we also know they have moved more laterally first, shifting the weight onto the front leg. (Notice the elevated right heels.)

It now starts becoming very obvious that not only are the unorthodox backswing professionals beginning to look the same at Position 4 but they also look the same as those who make technically correct backswings. *By the time the downswing is initiated, all the good ball strikers are essentially in the same position.*

Notice the similarities between John Daly and Greg Norman (above) and Fred Couples and Lee Janzen (below) as they swing into Position 4.

In the case of amateurs, who make unorthodox backswings similarly to some professionals but lack compensation skills, nothing can be done at this point in the downswing except to accept the consequences. The shaft angles that are above the plane, too steeply oriented, will result in the pull or slice. The shafts that are too shallow, too horizontally oriented, will usually result in hooks or pushes, although it is possible for the shallow-angled shaft to move out and across the original shaft angle plane in a similar manner as the too steeply angled shaft.

This is another area of the swing where I feel much emphasis has been placed on the clubhead's movement without appropriate concern for the movement of the other end. As the hands and butt end of the club move up in the last few positions of the backswing and then move back down in the initial stages of the downswing, they are moving on a diagonal line of a certain pitch.

The hands move up on line.

The hands move down on the same line.

Geometrically, this certainly makes sense, as we have seen the diagonal positioning of the shaft at address, at Position 2, and again at Position 4. In the correct motion, the hands and butt end of the club alsowork up and then down on a certain diagonal. Regardless of whether the golfer's hand line is on, under, or above this diagonal going back, it must be on it coming down. If not, the shaft will move out of position and become too steep or flat, resulting in an incorrect path of the clubhead at impact. Most golfers move the hand line well out as the hands, arms, and club descend. Usually, the clubhead will follow, again resulting in the outside-in path at impact. Better players, however, often make the same move; but as they do so, they move the clubhead back, flattening the shaft's position at this point. This is equally disastrous, as the clubhead approaches impact from too inside. I refer to the resulting impact position as *inside, steep* because the grip end of the club is up in too steep a position, relative to the angle it started on, as the clubhead swings inside-out. Severe pushes, blocks, and hooks result. Other players who hook or push the ball excessively also flatten the shaft too much here but drop the hand line down too vertically, under the proper diagonal hand line. The golf ball will still hook and push too much, but usually on a lower trajectory than that of the golfer who is inside, steep.

If you're having problems with your swing plane, be more aware of your hand line and what the movement of the grip end of the club is doing as you move down. Just as we saw in the takeaway, the butt end of the club moves on a prescribed arc (three dimensions) or diagonal (two dimensions) just as the clubhead does. I've found it has helped a lot of my students improve their swings who previously may have been focusing too much on just the clubhead's movement. There are drills and practice procedures that I will describe to help you with this aspect of the swing. For now, however, realize that controlling the movement of the butt end of the club assists you in controlling the movement of the clubhead itself.

The last position before impact is what I call *Position 5,* when the shaft again returns to a position that is parallel to the ground. As in Position 1, the shaft is parallel to the stance and target lines; but instead of being opposite the ball of the right foot, it is now out slightly, directly over the stance line.

Let me explain why this is so and why there's a difference between Positions 1 and 5. In Position 1, the swing is proceeding relatively slowly, and the right side of the body's rotational movement, although minimal, is inward as the club is moving back. In Position 5, however, the right side of the body is rotating outward and dynamically at a much greater rate of speed. It makes sense to me that the shaft would not be in the same location when the body is turning slowly rearward and the arms are moving slowly than when the body is turning rapidly outward and the arms are also rapidly swinging. Coming down, the shaft is slightly out more, that is, from ball of foot line to the toe line. This also explains why it is acceptable for the butt end of the club to be *slightly* elevated at impact compared to its starting position.

As we examine other features of this position, some things are worth noting: The left wrist is flat and in line with forearm. The clubface is square, again angled slightly downward, parallel to the spine angle. The right heel may be off the ground here, but it doesn't have to be. In

As Greg Norman swings through Position 5, you can see from the flex in the clubshaft how much more active, or dynamic, this position is compared to Position 1.

either case, the hips have moved laterally forward enough to shift the body weight from the right side to left and are now beginning to rotate more as they move uninterrupted on their prescribed arc. Therefore, the hips are already approximately 20 degrees open to the target. The shoulders, however, are well behind the movement of the hips so that they are virtually square at this point. Also note that the angle between the shaft and the left arm is still maintained, as it is only here that the wrists and forearms begin the process called *release*.

We are now a millisecond away from impact, our most important position. However, if you are good here at Position 5, it will be difficult not to apply a precise and accurate blow to the golf ball.

Impact: The Golf Swing's Most Critical Position

Everything we do before striking the ball—from focusing on our target line to setting the clubface perpendicular to it—is for the sole purpose of promoting square, solid club-face-to-ball contact at our optimum attainable speed. That's why impact is the golf swing's most critical position.

If you were to study the impact positions of one hundred good ball strikers such as Greg Norman (shown above), they would all share these common traits: body weight predominantly on the forward leg, right heel slightly elevated, both arms extended (with elbows close together and pointing downward, toward each hip), the back of the left wrist straight and in line with the left forearm, both hands slightly in front of (or even with) the clubhead. The hips are open to approximately 30 degrees, and the shoulders are square or just slightly open.

At the precise moment of impact, the clubhead is traveling along the target line, not going left or right. It is also moving at optimum attainable speed; and it has approached the ball from the proper angle of descent, not too steep or shallow.

The clubface is square to the target, not open or closed. The ball is being struck in the center of the clubface.

Tiger Woods: A Model of Precision and Power

When Tiger strikes the ball, the vital signs involving body and club positions are perfect. This is one reason he's able to swing the club at a speed of around 125 miles per hour and consistently deliver the sweetspot of the club squarely into the ball.

The Grip: How You Place Your Hands on the Club Is Vitally Important

Whether you choose to play with an overlapping, interlocking, or ten-fingered grip is a personal choice. What really matters is the way your hands are united on the top of the club. The manner in which you hold the club here is a major factor in where its face is positioned at impact.

In assuming your left-hand grip, let the club rest diagonally across the fingers.

In assuming your right-hand grip, let the club rest diagonally across the fingers, primarily at the first joint up from the palm.

When completing the grip, the thumb of the left hand should rest just to the right of center on the club's handle. The greatest amount of pressure should be slightly on the thumb's right side, not directly on the pad.

For the right-handed player standing at address and looking down, the thumb and forefinger of the right hand should touch on the left side of the club.

What's most critical is that, when the hands are placed together as a unit, the vees formed by the thumb and forefinger of each hand point to a spot between your chin and right shoulder, depending on swing tendencies. Notice the vee of the right hand in this photograph.

Warning: Just Because a Bad Grip Feels Comfortable, Doesn't Mean You Will Deliver the Club Squarely into the Ball—Usually It Means Just the Opposite

Although there are pros who play quite successfully using unorthodox grips, understand that they hit hundreds of practice balls per day and have learned how to make corrective compensatory movements in their swings. Average golfers, with limited time to practice, put themselves at a disadvantage when they hold the club with an incorrect grip. Typically, players adopt a grip that feels comfortable, but is incorrect, and prevents them from delivering the clubface squarely to the ball. Please recognize that, at first, the correct placement of the hands on the club will feel neither natural nor comfortable. With repetition, however, the discomfort will soon go away.

Here *(above right)*, both hands are turned away from the target, in what is commonly called an exaggerated strong position. When standing at address, the right-handed player sees the vees point up to the right shoulder, or even farther right.

Many golfers who swing across the ball and slice adopt this grip as a countering measure. It helps close the clubface, and on occasion it can help. But the assistance this grip provides is inconsistent at best. Such a grip impedes the natural hinging of the wrists in the backswing. Furthermore, it will close the clubface excessively on chips, pitches, and sand shots, causing the ball to fly low and left of target.

Here *(below right)*, both hands are turned too far toward the target, in what is commonly called an exaggerated weak position. When standing at address, the right-handed player sees the vees pointing up between the chin and left ear.

The player who adopts such a grip dramatically opens, or fans, the clubface on the backswing, setting the clubface in a very open position at the top and arriving at impact with the clubface still open. This golfer often will swing down too aggressively, from outside-in to an exaggerated degree. This is in an effort to keep the ball from flying too far to the right. He or she may also try to rotate the forearms prematurely through impact, in an effort to keep the ball from flying far right of target. These measures are usually in vain, and contrary to proper swinging motion.

The Setup: Correct Posture Is Vital

Many golfers fail to realize the vital importance of this preswing fundamental. Good posture does four things: (1) It sets you up in a dynamic, athletic starting position, (2) it establishes your distance from the ball, (3) it sets you in position to turn your upper body against a resisting lower body; and (4) it encourages the arms and shoulders to move on the appropriate backswing and downswing planes.

In establishing proper posture, you tilt your straight spine forward from the hip joints; do not curve it forward from the waist. How much tilt depends on the club being swung; the spine is a little more inclined with a short iron than with a driver, but the difference is minimal.

Flex the knees slightly—a little more if you are particularly tall, over six foot, two for a man, five foot, nine for a woman. When the knees are flexed correctly and the tilt of the spine is sufficiently forward, the rear end moves back and out, counterbalancing the upper body's forward position. The result is that the body's weight, or center of gravity, is placed squarely and correctly on the balls of the feet, not the toes and certainly not the heels, which can occur when the knees are too bent.

When the upper body is tilted forward, the arms hang almost vertically downward, free and clear from the legs. The hands and butt end of the club will be about a hand's width away from the legs. This distance is a constant for all clubs, and it provides you ample freedom to swing the arms and club without hindrance from your body.

It is also imperative that the spine be tilted forward so the shoulders can turn on an inclined plane, which is essentially what the golf swing is—a circular motion on a plane that is tilted away from the ball.

Postural Problems: The Incorrect Tilt of the Spine Can Cause Major Swing Faults

If you stoop over and reach for the ball with your weight on the toes of your feet *(above left)* or sit back with your weight on your heels *(above right)*, you will turn the hips and shoulders incorrectly, swing the club on an incorrect path and plane, hit the ball off the toe or heel of the club and hit off-line shots. For these reasons, particularly, I advise you either to do spot checks of your address position in front of a mirror or to check your posture by looking at yourself on video.

Forming a mental picture of a tour player with good posture, such as Greg Norman *(left)* will encourage you to set up correctly.

It's important to recognize that you may be assuming an incorrect posture (i.e., weight on heels) because of a faulty swing (i.e., outside-in down) you have become familiar with. When you fix your posture at address, it becomes imperative that you also try to fix that aspect of your swing that led you to modify your postural position in the first place.

Position 1: Get It Right, to Better Your Chance of Being Correct at the Top and Returning the Club to a Solid Square Impact Position

At Position 1, shown here from the front view, the clubshaft is below my waist and parallel to the target line, as well as horizontal to the ground. The clubshaft is opposite the ball of my right foot, and the clubface is parallel to my spine angle. My right arm is visible above the left. My weight is already into the right leg, which remains flexed slightly at the knee. My shoulders have begun to turn, but only about 30 degrees of the full 90 degrees desired and only owing to the movement of the arms, not by any conscious effort. The wrists are beginning to hinge, but only because of the movement and weight of the clubhead.

Two Common Backswing Errors: These Two Mistakes Can Be Dangerous to Your Swinging Action

If an imaginary line is drawn along the golfer's clubshaft at address, we establish what is called the shaft angle plane. As the arms, hands, wrists, and shoulders start the club back, the clubhead is moving gradually upward and inward along this plane line. It is a proper blend of the in and up movements that allows the clubhead to swing on plane. But for this to happen, the butt end of the club needs to be moving in precisely the same manner as the clubhead, only on a smaller scale. The butt end should also move upward and inward on this same plane line.

Instead of letting the arms initiate the backswing and swing the club correctly to Position 1, many golfers manipulate the club with their

hands. As a result, they swing the clubhead either well under the shaft angle plane (represented by elongated yellow shaft), with the butt out *(top left),* or above the plane *(top right),* with the butt out.

When swinging back, you should strive for this on plane position *(above right).* Practice swinging to Position 1 regularly and check it frequently with the help of a mirror, video, or friend.

At the Top: If You Are Not in a Good Position, You Must Compensate as You Swing Down, Otherwise a Good Shot Will Not Ensue

When you reach the top of the swing, you are only about one-half second from impact. Therefore, you don't have much time to fix a faulty position.

Although there is some latitude in defining what is the correct at-the-top position, most powerfully accurate players share these elements:

- The left arm is straight, but not rigid.
- The left wrist is straight and in line with the left forearm.
- The right arm is away from the side, the forearm is approximately parallel to the spine, and the upper arm is parallel to the ground.
- The shoulders are on an angle consistent with the tilt of the upper body, established originally at address.
- The hands are above the height of the right shoulder.
- The clubface is square-angled downward, and approximately—if not exactly—parallel to the left arm and wrist.
- The clubshaft is parallel to the target line (if it was swung back far enough at the top to be parallel to the ground).

Unorthodox or Classic: Which At-the-Top Position Is Better?

Lee Trevino is one of the all-time accurate drivers of a golf ball. However, he has a personalized swing that was grooved by hitting thousands of golf balls. See for yourself how different his unorthodox backswing *(left)* looks compared to Lee Janzen's classic at-the-top position *(right)*.

The more technically correct your backswing position is, the better your chance of delivering the clubface squarely to the ball at impact. Therefore, unless you have a great pair of hands, supreme feel for the clubhead, superior eye-hand coordination, and hours and hours to devote to practice, it's better to try to groove a top-of-backswing position similar to Janzen's.

Attention Hookers and Slicers: These Two Simple Drills Can Help Cure Your Errant Shots

Many golfers who hook the ball, swing the club back and down too far inside the target line, and close the face too early coming into impact. To correct these swing faults, practice hitting shots with the ball below your feet. This drill allows you to instinctively swing on a more upright plane and make the proper adjustments necessary for delivering the clubface squarely to the ball.

If your bad shot is a slice, you may be taking the club back either on an excessively flat or overly steep plane, then coming over the top down with the club swinging across the target line and ball with an open face. To fix this fault, practice hitting shots with the ball above your feet. This drill automatically allows you to swing into impact on a shallower plane.

The "Buddy" System: You Can Correct Two Common Backswing Faults with the Help of a Friend

If you're hitting weak shots, it could be because you are straightening your right knee on the backswing. This is a common fault that disrupts the weight shift and coiling actions of the body, draining power from your swing.

To correct this fault, have a friend hold your right knee firmly to keep its flex as you swing back. This drill helps you get a feel for shifting your weight onto your right foot and leg and leveraging your right heel into the ground.

If you are swinging the club too inside-out or outside-in and hitting off-line shots, have a friend squat behind you and hold a clubshaft directly above an extension of your stance line. Swing the club back to waist height, trying to position the shaft parallel to the ground and above the other shaft. Practicing this drill a few times, holding the position for a few seconds each time, should help you straighten out your problem.

Mind Over Matter: Visualizing a Good Downswing Helps You Employ the Correct Movements of the Body and Club

Once you intellectually understand the vital positions of the downswing described in this book, study the photographs here, taking a few minutes to implant them into your mind's eye. Look at each photograph individually, then imagine them coming alive as a sequence. You'll soon realize, as you practice and play, how much this visual practice pays off.

Postimpact: Matching This Key Position Can Improve Your Downswing

Many golfers underestimate the value of learning and grooving good postimpact positions. They feel that since these positions are attained after the ball has already been hit, that they are not important. The fact is, I believe you can actually improve a poor downswing by working on the critical through swing positions; in other words, improve your swing in reverse order.

For example, take a player who swings on an exaggerated inside-out path. The club drops too far under the correct plane in the downswing; then at impact and beyond the clubhead swings out too much, too far to the right of the target. Furthermore, the arms separate out too far away from the body. By improving the correct direction of movement of the arms and club in the through swing, the player will be forced to correct the downswing plane to be successful.

If you have this problem, study this photograph, which shows how both arms extend and the upper part of the left arm stays glued to the left chest area. The Simulated Impact Drill described in Chapter 2 can also help you solve certain downswing problems.

How to Stop Blocking: This Drill Helps You Feel That the Club Is Too Far Behind You, Cures Improper Lower Body Motion, and Stops Shots Hit Right of Target

If you vigorously slide your legs too much toward the target on the downswing, you probably block shots out to the right. That's because, when you exaggerate the lateral movement of the legs, it's difficult to swing the clubhead correctly along the target line at impact. It is traveling out too far to the right.

To cure this problem, place an old clubshaft several inches to the left of the heel of your front foot *(below left)*. Make your normal backswing. Start the downswing by letting the left hip move slightly laterally. As the body and arms move to impact, the left hip then moves rotationally just enough to move weight onto the left leg. Make sure your arms fall in conjunction with this move, with the club shaft dropping to an inside parallel position. This rotational hip movement is an important link to squaring the clubface.

If you employ the correct downswing movement, your left hip will gently brush the shaft in front of your foot (instead of crashing into it), before rotating to the left *(below right)*.

An incorrect tendency I see with fixing this problem is for players to attempt to rotate or clear the left hip excessively fast, leaving the club and arms too far behind. Another problem you can fall into as you correct your hip motion is to move the hands and club out initially as you start down, rather than let them fall. The better player will do this in an effort to swing left. Then, in mid-downswing, the clubhead will try to move back in and behind, though the hands have moved outward. The result is a block anyway, as the hands and butt end of the club return to an overly high position at impact. This is true, even though the clubhead may have returned to an acceptable path.

On the Money: When the Hard Work Pays Off

There is nothing more pleasurable to a golfer than seeing his or her shot fly powerfully at the intended target. The secret is to practice sensibly and diligently, so that on-target shots become a regular occurrence. It's also important to know your swing inside and out, so that when something goes wrong you know how to fix it. But remember, even the game's best players don't hit good shots all of the time.

CHAPTER 5

The Through Swing

Conventional thinking in golf says the through swing, that part of the swing after impact, is a natural consequence of all the movements that precede it . . . that if your setup, backswing, at-the-top position, and downswing are good, the through swing (or follow-through) will be good as well. It will simply take care of itself. In fact, you might even hear a great player say he or she never thinks about anything in the swing after impact.

To some extent this is true, but not totally. It's a bit of an oversimplification that can actually interfere with some players' improvement in their swings. In the real world of golf, there are several other scenarios that relate to the through swing and often are overlooked.

There is the example of an excellent swinger who is good at address, good in the backswing, good at impact, and good in the follow through. And at the other end of the spectrum is the golfer who is poor in all the swing positions before the through swing and who is also poor, as we would expect, in the through swing itself.

Grooving good postimpact positions is much more vital than the average golfer thinks.

However, other combinations very definitely exist. There's the player whose swing is technically incorrect going back, wrong at the top, a little better starting down, then quite good at impact and in the follow through. You certainly could not say the poor early positions created the good later ones in a cause-and-effect manner. I have worked with amateur students who exhibit this type of swing. However, it may surprise you to know that some tour players fall into this category, too.

Occasionally I see the player whose swing is good back, good at the top, and even good starting down. It may even look good right up to impact, or just a fraction before. Then, surprisingly, some component of the swing begins to break down at this precise moment, resulting in some aspect of the through swing being quite poor.

I cited one such example in Chapter 2. A student swings into what appears to be an acceptable impact position, but poor postimpact positions revealed this was not the case. The student may have looked okay at impact; but dynamically, the process of breaking down the left wrist and arm was beginning.

Another example involves the movement of the lower body. All looks good in the backswing and downswing, but just after impact it becomes apparent the shifting of weight and the rotating of the body were prematurely slowing. Such dynamics would be imperceptible, even using a video camera, until the swing reaches the postimpact stages. At this point it becomes obvious: An excessive amount of weight remains on the back foot, the hips and shoulders have failed to rotate completely to a full finish; and there is too much space between the knees. Instead of the body accelerating continuously from the top to a complete finish, it begins to slow too soon.

A final example of an early good swing showing an incorrect postimpact position comes from the better player who has strong hands, wrists, and forearms. Again, setup, backswing, and downswing all look fine. Impact may appear to look good also. But just past impact, it becomes evident that the forearms have been rotating correctly, but way too fast. The correct rate of rotation that results from a more natural release has been interfered with. Again, the faulty process began just before impact, but it does not become evident until afterward.

Poor shots result because the dynamics of the club's movement during impact are being compromised. More precisely, the face is opening, or closing, too rapidly. Also, the clubhead's path, speed, or both are being altered. The bottom line: The laws of impact are being adversely influenced.

Certainly, in the examples given, the students were not able to rely on the quality of their backswings and downswings to create a dynamically correct impact and follow through. Unfortunately for them, it didn't happen. The corrective action, therefore, is to modify and correct the through swing so the dynamics of the club's movement through impact does not deteriorate. This can be done, usually rather easily, by working on various drills, such as the Simulated Impact Drill, presented in Chapter 2.

A discussion such as this also raises the question of whether you can improve a poor swing in reverse order. In other words, can you improve a downswing by working on the through swing, and can you improve a backswing by just working on the downswing? I certainly think so. If there is any truth to the concept that a good follow through can be the product of a good backswing and downswing—and this is certainly the case for some players—certainly the opposite could be true. And it is. I have seen it happen with a number of students for whom I have adapted this approach.

An example of improving a backswing by just working on the downswing is the following: A player starts the club back, either on plane or above it; then he or she lifts it up abruptly in swinging to the top. The downswing is too steep and from outside-in. By just working on the downswing, doing drills to shallow the downswing plane so the path becomes more from the inside, the backswing gradually, indirectly, reacts to the intentions of the downswing. It begins to shallow, too. No direct, conscious effort is directed to the backswing, but it gradually changes on its own.

An example of improving a downswing by working on the through swing is shown by a player who swings on an exaggerated inside-out path. The club drops too far under the correct plane in the downswing; then at impact and beyond, the clubhead swings out too much, too far to the right of the target. The arms separate out too far away from the body as well. By working just on the correct direction of movement of the arms and club in the through swing, the player will gradually correct the downswing plane.

Let's now look at the movement of the body, arms, and club in the through swing and see what constitutes correct motion.

As I mentioned in Chapter 2 when describing the Simulated Impact Drill, I want the student to hold the postimpact position, which is short, with the left hand swinging no more than eighteen inches past impact. At this point in a full swing, the left arm will be absolutely straight (as will be the right) with the shaft, left wrist, and arm all essentially forming a straight line. The upper portion of the left arm is still tight to the left chest area. Even though the forearms, wrists, and clubshaft are in the process of rotating, the back of the left hand is pointing only *slightly* downward toward the ground. A slicer would have the back of the left hand pointing upward toward the sky to some degree, and one who has an overly aggressive turnover would have it pointing much more downward toward the ground at this position.

The weight of the body is now well into the left leg, which, as it receives the weight from the right side, is in the process of straightening.

In this early postimpact position, the right heel is well off the ground and the right knee has moved inward.

This is important, since it is this bracing of the leg that causes the left hip to stop its lateral movement forward and start rotating vigorously, clearing to the left. The bracing process helps you generate power and swing the club along the desired path to the target with your arms. In addition, it prevents the upper body, particularly the head and right shoulder, from dropping excessively in the downswing, causing fat shots. The right heel is well off the ground at this position, and the right knee is moving forward. Because the hips are rotating and the right heel has been released from the ground, the right knee is being *pulled* into this position—an important concept to grasp: the player is not artificially and exaggeratedly thrusting the right knee forward, which causes the upper body to fall back into what is called an excessive *reverse C position*. The hips, which were already 45 degrees or so open at impact, are now more open as they proceed with a continuous rotational movement all the way to the finish. The shoulders are also now open at about 30 degrees

At this point in the through swing, all great ball strikers look virtually identical.

or so. They are not quite as open to the target as the hips, but they are catching up.

The next important through swing position, shown in the photograph at left, is when the right arm has swung forward and up enough to reach a position parallel to the ground, or just slightly beyond. No matter what their differences might have been before this position, all great ball strikers look virtually identical here. Two players who you might think would be exceptions because of their finishes are Arnold Palmer and Justin Leonard. Palmer has an unorthodox, high hold-on look, whereas Leonard has the very low collapsed arm appearance. In the postimpact position, however, they are no different from other great ball strikers. Conclusion? These players' finishes are simply artificial concoctions that have no cause-and-effect relationship with prior positions. They both may *think* or *feel* their finishes somehow have some influence on their ball striking, but it is basically cosmetic maneuvering at this point.

As we examine this postimpact position, we'll see that the right arm is fully extended. It is precisely here that the forearms, wrists, and hands are fully and completely rotated. The back of the left hand is well underneath the right, pointing well downward toward the ground. The left arm is now beginning to fold slightly at the elbow, because the left hand is closer to the body than is the right. Even though the arm is slightly bent, the elbow is pointing downward, toward the left hip, and not backward or outward behind the player, which is the case with many golfers. Such an arm position is called the *chicken wing*, and I see it far too often. The upper left arm, which was against the side in the prior position discussed, has now moved away from the side as the right arm extends. At this point we also see the wrists rehinging, so that the shaft is pointing upward on an angle, approximating the original shaft angle established at address.

I think it is of interest to note here the symmetrical nature of different positions of the golf swing. For example, if your perception of this through swing position is a little unclear, I ask you to recall its mirror image position in the backswing, a position with which you are probably much more familiar. In Chapter 3 I identified it as Position 2. The left arm is straight, the right arm is folded at the elbow, and the elbow is away from the side. The wrists are at some stage in their hinging

When watching yourself swing on video, if you see your left arm in these faulty chicken wing positions, employing poor arm extension, the Simulated Impact Drill will help you tremendously.

process, and the clubshaft is pointing upward, on an angle that approximates the original shaft angle at address. The through swing position is practically identical, although the amount of wrist hinge and the plane angle of the shaft may vary a bit. The important point, however, is that the positions are so similar you can examine one to learn much about the other. Look back at Position 2 and see for yourself.

We now move on to the swing's final position; and again, as you might expect, as different as good swings may look in previous positions, the finish of a golf swing is strikingly similar among expert players. If you need confirmation, look at the finish positions of John Daly and Greg Norman.

Starting from the ground up, the right foot has come up completely

Look how similar John Daly's (left) *and Greg Norman's* (right) *final positions are.*

and rotated 90 degrees forward. The shoelaces are facing the target. The weight of the body has moved to the outside, rear portion of the left foot, so that the left instep may be slightly elevated off the ground. The left leg is straight and the right is folded at the knee, so the right knee is very close to, if not touching, the left. This indicates a full release of the body's right side and a complete rotation of the hips, so they are at the very least facing parallel left of the target. The hips of most great ball strikers rotate even farther around than this. The finish position of the shoulders is even more fully rotated, the right shoulder much closer to the target than is the left. Most important, the body in perfect balance, indicating a beautiful blend of power and control.

One of the important elements of balance is that the upper body has rotated to a finish over the left leg. The head and right shoulder are directly above the left leg, or possibly slightly behind the leg if the hips have driven more laterally in the downswing. The right shoulder can raise some from impact to finish; but for most players, the right shoulder is still slightly lower than the left when the swing is complete. Some great ball strikers, who are exceptions, finish with the shoulders level; but I do not recommend this for the recreational player. For those of you who finish off the ball with the right shoulder higher than the left, this is a tip that you were outside-in coming down. The shape of the swing is the cause of the raising of the shoulder. It will do you no good to try to force yourself to stay down in this instance. The plane of the downswing must be corrected first.

The finish position of the arms is very relaxed and natural; the hands and club are behind the head. Both arms are now folded at the elbows, yet the club is still fully controlled. The hands finish approximately level with the left ear and above the left shoulder area.

If, for any reason, you do not finish correctly, I highly recommend you execute the *Start at the Finish Drill* to improve this aspect of your swing. As we discussed earlier, you may soon find that by doing this,

Know the difference between a good and bad finish. Here, for example, the upper body is leaning too far away from the target, indicating that an insufficient amount of weight was shifted over to the left foot and leg. The position of the hands is too high as well.

you will correct swing faults that occurred earlier in your swing. For this drill, pose yourself in as absolutely perfect a finish position as you can. Complete a backswing slowly, then swing forward smoothly, returning to the position from which you began, the finish. When you swing backward, go all the way to the top of the backswing, then in a continuous motion, swing down and through to the finish. Go slowly at first until you feel control and balance. You may be a little out of balance at first, but that's okay. Keep doing the drill until the body finds good balance, which it will. This is a wonderful drill for curing many swing ailments such as incomplete use of the body, hitting at the ball rather than through it, finishing out of balance (for example, the upper body moving too far forward toward the target at the finish), and coordinating the arm swing motion with the movement of the body.

The golf swing is now complete. Let's now look at a starting position that encourages the swing's most sound execution.

Start at the final drill.

Put yourself in as perfect a finish position as you can.

Swing back to the top.

Swing from the top back to your starting position.

CHAPTER 6

Preswing Fundamentals

You cannot set up to the golf ball any way you please and expect to execute a sound swing with any degree of consistency. There is an optimum starting position that involves five elements, often identified as the preswing fundamentals:

1. Grip
2. Stance
3. Posture
4. Ball position
5. Alignment

The starting position is also referred to as the setup or address position, and its importance cannot be overlooked or overemphasized. If it is good—if it is fundamentally correct—you have given yourself the chance to make a good swing. There is no guarantee you will do so, but at least you have given yourself the chance.

The basic setup position for a 5 iron. In the photo on the left, I'm on a slightly uphill lie.

Conversely, if your setup is poor, you basically have guaranteed your swing will not be correct. You might hit an acceptable shot, but only on occasion and not with any degree of consistency.

Out of every hundred amateur golfers I see, no more than two or three execute all the preswing fundamentals correctly. Conversely, this is another area of commonality among the professionals and great ball strikers. Although their swings reflect individual characteristics, it is of great importance to note how similar they all look at address. Their grips are not all the same, and in a few cases not even conventional; however, most have worked extremely hard on the placement of their hands on the club, in a position that would be identified as "neutral."

Good players who employ a slightly stronger or weaker grip do so primarily because of ball flight preference—they prefer a draw or fade or a lower or higher trajectory. The few whose grips are considered too strong or too weak have made swing compensations that are compatible, or what I would identify as acceptable variations. These few great players should be viewed for what they are, however. They are exceptions to the rule and should not be used as examples to justify an incorrect grip of your own.

Instead, look at the majority of great ball strikers and see how perfectly and beautifully they place their hands on a golf club. I am reminded of Harvey Penick's wonderful line: "Bad grip, bad swing." For him, it was that simple. You employ an incorrect grip, your swing must adjust to compensate—and such adjustments will be incorrect as well.

Regarding the other four preswing fundamentals employed by the best ball strikers, you will see even less deviation than in their grips. Alignment, ball position, stance, and posture are, for the most part, perfect. When they are not, it is by mistake, not design. That is why these variables are constantly monitored by the good player, who knows minute changes may not be noticed right away. As inconsequential as the slight deviation may seem, he or she also knows the influence on the swing can be devastating.

Let's look at each of the five preswing fundamentals more closely.

If you set up incorrectly (left), *your chances of consistently achieving good positions through the hitting area* (right) *are remote.*

Grip

Obviously, the size of all golfers' hands and the length of all golfers' fingers are not the same. Therefore, everyone's hands are not going to fit onto a golf grip in exactly the same way. In addition, the wrist position at the top of the backswing is an influencing component to the grip. The size of the grip installed on the shaft can also be adjusted slightly for hands that are exceptionally large or small. However, that being said, such variations should relate more to what one's grip looks like on the underneath side, not on top. In other words, hand size, grip size, finger length, and even the strength and flexibility of the fingers and wrists can determine whether you might use an overlapping, interlocking, or ten-fingered grip. That decision is more personal preference. I am infinitely more concerned with how your hands look on top of the club, and it is here we must see correct positioning and more uniformity among players. Before reviewing the elements of a good grip, let me first mention some of the common incorrect ones. Again, golfers will not give themselves the best chance of returning the club to a square position at impact if they assume any one of these grips.

Weak Left Hand, Strong Right Hand

The golfer who rotates the left hand too far to the left, or counterclockwise, usually is holding the club too much in the palm and often claims this grip feels more secure. I believe this is a false sensation. The player who assumes such a grip sees only one knuckle of the left hand when at address looking down. The back of the hand points directly parallel to the ground. The vee formed between the thumb and forefinger points straight up or even left of the golfer's chin; although the vee is often difficult to distinguish, because the thumb is usually separated away from the inside base of the forefinger. Combined with a strong right hand (hand turned too much clockwise), the left thumb is totally visible to the golfer, which it should not be. If the right hand were more on top of the club, rather than too far to the side, the left thumb would fit neatly into the palm of the right hand and would not be visible.

The strong right hand is rotated too far right, or clockwise, from the golfer's perspective. This means the grip end of the club is resting too

A very exaggerated weak left hand, strong right hand grip (from the player's visual perspective).

much in the palm of the hand as well, similar to the left. If not into the palm, it is at least too much across the base of the fingers, rather than across the second joint, such that the fingertips cannot rest securely against the left side of the club's grip as they should. The right-hand vee would point at best to the golfer's right shoulder but more often than not would entirely miss the body.

With a grip such as this, the hands are opposing each other, instead of being unified as a single link. The left hand wants to open the clubface excessively during the swing; the right hand wants to close it. Where it is at impact depends on some other variables, such as the plane of the downswing; but usually the left hand wins. The clubface fans open in the takeaway, leading to an over-the-top downswing and a slice. Occasionally, however, the strong right hand may dominate in the downswing and close the face, resulting in pulls or pull-hooks.

The player who holds the club with even a moderate weak left hand, strong right hand grip will often fan the clubface open on the backswing.

Weak Left Hand, Weak Right Hand

In the weak left hand, weak right hand grip, both hands are turned so far counterclockwise that the vees formed by the thumb and forefinger of each hand point at the golfer's chin, if not left of it. This grip promotes a very open clubface at the top and, consequently, a very open clubface at impact. This golfer will often swing down too aggressively, swing down from outside-in to an exaggerated degree, and often will develop premature rotation of the forearms through impact, all in an effort to keep the ball from flying far right of target. This effort is usually in vain. With such an open-face, the worst shot with an iron will be a shank, which will occur not infrequently.

Strong Left Hand, Weak Right Hand

This grip combines a weak right hand position with a strong left, the vee of which points, at best, to the right shoulder but usually beyond. The golfer can see all four knuckles as the back of the left hand points diagonally skyward. I see the strong left hand, weak right hand grip more often than you might think; it is, for many, quite natural. It is identical to the position the hands are in when the arms are hanging down naturally, palms turned inward on both hands. Again, we have hands in conflict—this time the right

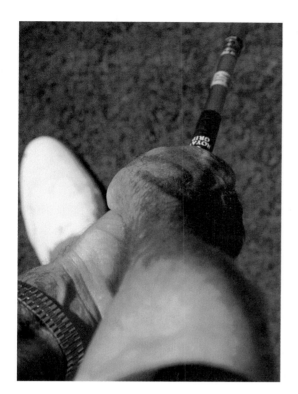

A very exaggerated weak left hand, weak right hand grip (from the player's visual perspective).

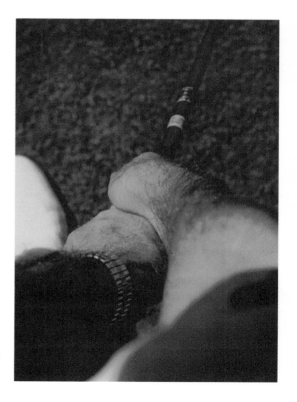

The strong left hand, weak right hand grip (from the player's visual perspective).

hand wants to open the clubface and the left hand is in a position to close it. On any given swing either can win, though there are too few occasions when, at impact, the clubface is square. I believe, on average, the right hand position usually predominates, causing the clubface to open excessively in the backswing and ultimately stay too open at impact.

Strong Left Hand, Strong Right Hand

Many golfers who are severely outside-in down, and who consequently slice, adopt the strong left hand, strong right hand grip as a countering measure. It helps close the otherwise too open clubface, and in fact, on occasion can help. But this grip is a classic example of one fault correcting another, and the assistance such a grip provides is inconsistent at best. In addition, such a grip impedes the natural hinging of the wrists in the backswing. And while it may help the full swing occasionally, it is very detrimental to the short game closing the clubface for chips, pitches, and sand shots, causing the ball to go too low and left of target.

John Daly (left) *and Fred Couples* (right) *both use the strong left hand, strong right hand grip. Understand, however, that they have the unique talent to make the necessary swing compensations. The typical club-level player would be smart to assume a more neutral grip, unless he or she has a severe slice.*

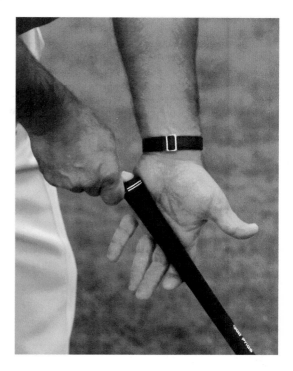

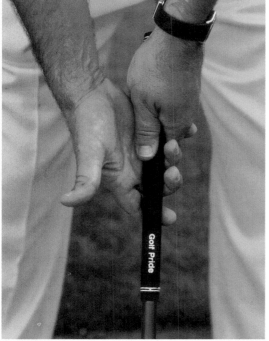

Assuming a neutral grip (above, left) *involves setting the club diagonally in the left hand* (above, right) *as well as in the right hand* (below, left).

Model Grip

How is the club held more correctly? The grip of the club rests diagonally across the fingers of the left hand. When closed, the thumb is just to the right of center on the grip; the greatest amount of pressure is slightly to the thumb's right side, not directly on the pad. The left-hand vee points between the golfer's chin and right shoulder. The grip rests across the middle of the fingers of the right hand. When closed, the fingertips are on the club. The thumb and forefinger touch at their sides on the left side of the club. The right-hand vee points to the same location as that of the left.

Please recognize that, at first, a correct placement of the hands on a golf club will feel neither natural nor comfortable. With repetition, however, the discomfort will soon go away, and you can then be sure your grip will not prevent you from acquiring a sound golf swing.

Stance

Stance simply refers to the placement of the feet—both the position of the feet and their distance apart. The commonly accepted barometer for distance apart is the width of the shoulders or hips—slightly wider for the driver and longer-shafted clubs, slightly narrower for short irons. This is a good starting point, as long as we recognize there are acceptable variations, particularly in regard to one's swing type. For example, a wide stance is not good for a golfer who has difficulty shifting weight to the right side in the backswing. A slightly narrower stance than normal makes the task easier. The same could be said for shifting weight in the downswing. A narrower stance can also be good for the golfer who overswings at the top of the backswing, as it tends to tone down the extent of arm swing for some. Conversely, the taller player usually needs a slightly wider base than the person of more average height. I also like to encourage a wider stance for a player who is not aggressive enough in his or her downswing speed. Women definitely tend to have a stance that is too narrow, men do so occasionally. Men tend to have a stance that is too

Notice how my stance for the driver (left) *is slightly wider than my stance for the 5 iron* (right).

wide, women quite rarely. A stance that is too narrow creates instability, particularly in the backswing. Weight can too easily shift to the outside of the foot, causing it to roll outward. Checking your stance width in a mirror can be very enlightening. If you discover it is too wide, hit some balls with your feet together, literally touching one another. Subsequently, when you widen to a correct distance, it won't feel too uncomfortable.

There is leeway for the positioning of the feet as well. Generally, the right foot should be perpendicular to the target line, the left foot angled outward, toward the target, about 30 degrees. If the left foot is turned outward too much, it will restrict your ability to fully turn your hips and shoulders in the backswing. It will also allow the left leg to drift too far forward in the downswing, encouraging pushes and hooks. A good corrective is to practice hitting balls with your left foot perpendicular to the target line. From there, when you turn the foot out the proper amount, it won't feel so restrictive.

The left foot is turned out to allow the left leg and foot to receive the body's weight in the through swing, without undue stress to the ankle.

The position of the right foot can be modified somewhat, depending on your flexibility and consequent ability to achieve a full shoulder turn in the backswing. If such flexibility and turn are lacking, turning the right foot out a maximum of 40 degrees is an acceptable modification. Otherwise, the right foot should be perpendicular to the target line. A right foot that is turned inward has the same restrictive effect on the backswing as a left foot that is turned too far out.

Posture

Many amateur golfers fail to understand the importance of posture as a preswing fundamental. For this reason, they rarely think of tracing faulty backswing and downswing positions to bad posture at address. Don't make the same mistake. Set up correctly with good posture, to encourage good swing positions.

Good posture does four things. First, it sets you up in a dynamic, athletic starting position, not unlike a position akin to other sports. The golf swing should be dynamic and athletic, and you must begin this way if you want your swing to incorporate such characteristics. Second, proper posture establishes your distance from the ball. The ball may move in or out, depending on the club you are swinging, but a constant is your arm hang and how far from your left leg your left hand is at address. Third, correct posture separates the upper body from the lower, so that you can turn your upper body against a lower body that resists. This gives you maximum coil and power. Fourth, correct posture assists your arms and shoulders in moving on appropriate planes in the backswing and downswing, which gives you the best opportunity to swing the club up and down on the correct planes as well. That's quite a lot involved for just one component of the preswing procedure.

In proper posture, a straight spine is tilted forward at the hip joints, not curved forward at the waist. How much tilt depends on the club being swung, but though your spine is a little more inclined with a short iron than with a driver, the difference is minimal. However, most of the

Bad posture, at address, can lead to faulty backswing positions (above, left and right) *and bad downswing positions, such as the one shown here* (left).

responsibility for lowering the clubhead to the ground is that of the tilting forward of the spine, not the bending of the knees, which is far too common. For this reason, as I mentioned in Chapter 1, I never use the phrases Bend the knees and Sit on a stool.

I believe you should flex the knees slightly—a little more if you are particularly tall, over 6'2" for a man and 5'9" for a woman. When the knees are overbent, the lower spine is pulled inward, the upper spine moves backward, and the spine ends up being too vertically oriented. When the knees are flexed and the tilt of the spine is sufficiently forward, the rear end moves back and out, counterbalancing the upper body's forward position. The net result is placing the body's weight, or center of gravity, squarely and correctly on the balls of the feet, not the toes and certainly not the heels, which can occur when the knees are too bent.

When the upper body is tilted forward, the arms will hang almost vertically downward, free and clear from the legs. The hands and butt end of the club will then be about a hand's width away from the legs, about four inches. With the knees too bent and the spine, therefore, not tilted enough, the arms will hang too close to the legs, or the golfer will artificially lift them out. This hand's-width distance, of butt end of club to left leg, is a constant for all clubs. That being the case, the distance you stand from the ball is basically established. This postured position is very much like a baseball infielder or a football linebacker anticipating the coming play. I also like the image of a tennis player preparing to receive a serve—chin up, spine tilted forward at the hips, springy and athletic on the balls of the feet.

Because of the tilting at the hips, as the shoulders turn in the backswing, the lower body is in a position to resist, which is desirable. If the upper and lower body are in too much of a straight line relationship, the hips will tend to overturn or even turn as much as the shoulders. Then an overswing is likely, as is a severe loss of power owing to insufficient coiling.

Last, as we have seen, the plane the club swings on is a key fundamental to the success of a golf swing. Anatomically, the shoulders turn on a 90 degree angle to the spine. If the spine is vertical, the shoulders will turn horizontally. Since the golf swing is not a horizontal motion, it is imperative the spine be tilted forward so the shoulders can turn on an

When it comes to learning the fundamentals of good posture—especially the correct spine tilt—Greg Norman is a superb model.

inclined plane, which is what a golf swing is. The arms and shoulders do not swing on identical planes, however. The arms swing on a plane that is more upright. The more horizontal the shoulder turn is, the more difficult it is to accomplish this. The more tilted the shoulder turn is, up to a point, the more the arms will be encouraged to swing correctly on plane.

An excellent procedure to work on posture is to hold a golf club and stand with your profile to a mirror. Start in the at attention position— legs and spine straight, chin up, shoulders back, arms folded at the sides—with the shaft of your club perfectly vertical like your spine. Keeping your legs straight, tilt your clubshaft and spine forward the same amount, about 30 degrees. Tilt at the hip joints. Your rear end should move back as your upper body moves forward. Next, drop the arms and club down so the clubhead descends to the ground or floor. Last, flex the knees slightly with weight on the balls of the feet. As the knees flex, they will move toward your hands, but not closer or farther away than a hand's width. Do this over and over until proper posture becomes second nature to you.

Ball Position

Ball position is usually indicated with reference to the position of the feet, particularly the left heel. This can be a little misleading, as everyone's stance is not the same width. If everyone were told to play the driver off the left heel, for example, a person with a wider than normal stance would have this ball position farther forward from the center of his or her body than one whose stance was narrower than normal. I would rather you use the reference of the base of the left arm, or armpit, for the driver's ball position. This is the correct position for this club and will always be a constant, no matter what the width of stance. Generally, those who cut across the ball with an outside-in motion will move the ball forward from its correct position. Because the bottom of the swing arc moves forward with this type of motion, the golfer simply moves the ball forward as well. Conversely, the exaggerated inside-out swing has the bottom of the arc move rearward toward the back foot. Again, the simple fix, though a wrong one, is to move the ball back as well.

The problem with these kinds of adjustments is that, again, the golfer is fixing one fault with another. In fact, if the ball is moved out of position to accommodate an incorrect swing, the player must continue making that incorrect swing if he or she wants any chance at all to make acceptable contact. The opposite scenario, however, can be used as an excellent swing improvement drill.

If you are an outside-in slicer, try hitting some shots literally off your back foot. The only way you can make solid contact is to alter your downswing plane so that the clubhead is approaching the ball more from the inside. With the outside-in swing, you would miss the ball altogether. Such a drastic alteration is what is sometimes needed to effect change in one's swing, though it need be only temporary; just long enough to acquire the feel of a better motion. Then the ball can be moved forward to a more correct position.

The opposite drill is equally good for those whose swing is inside-out and who have moved the ball back too far to accommodate. Move the ball well forward, past your left shoulder, and try hitting some 5 irons from this position. To contact the ball, you will feel a downswing plane that is closer to correct than the plane you have been on.

For the driver, then, the best ball position for the average player is off the left armpit. With a stance that is slightly wider than the shoulders, this places the ball just inside the left heel. For irons, I prefer the center of the stance to just slightly left of center for the recreational golfer. It is here that the golfer has the best chance of hitting the ball with a proper descending blow *and* a clubhead that is traveling along the correct path. Depending on lie, fairway woods can be played anywhere from the iron position to several inches more forward, but rarely as far forward as the driver. The tighter the lie the more the fairway wood should be pinched, similar to a descending blow with an iron. The more the ball is sitting up, the farther it can be moved forward and swept.

To visually appreciate varying ball positions, take another look at the photographs of me taking my stance for a driver and a 5 iron, shown earlier in this chapter.

Alignment

Alignment is the positioning of the body relative to the target and the target line. The critical factors are, first, the relationship of the different lines of the body relative to one another and, second, the relationship of those lines to the target line. The different lines of the body are the lines of the feet, knees, hips, forearms, shoulders, and eyes. Ideally, each of these lines are parallel to one another. When you are in a position referred to as *square,* these lines are all parallel to the target line, which means they all point slightly left of the target. From this position, the human body has the best chance of swinging a golf club on plane on both sides of the body, with power and accuracy.

Unfortunately, most golfers do not start from this position. Many players devote too much attention to the stance line only, erroneously thinking that if the foot line is correct, the rest of the body lines will be

correct too. In fact, it is quite easy to have a discrepancy between the foot line and one or more of the other body lines. In addition, in prioritizing the body lines, the foot line is not the most important; the shoulder line is. So, whereas most people are overly concerned with the stance line and still often fail to place this correctly, my preference is that they be more concerned with the shoulder line. The arms are attached to the shoulders, and the shoulders should be parallel to the target line to give the arms their best chance of swinging the clubhead along that line at impact. Ideally, however, all the lines of the body are parallel to the target line.

Many golfers have the shoulders open to the foot line. This is a very natural mistake resulting from the way they position the right hand and arm at address. It's very easy to allow the right shoulder to move out in this process. The problem is that this starting position encourages an outside-in swinging motion. If the golfer then makes the added mistake of moving the ball forward to accommodate this swing, the shoulders open even more at address as he or she places the clubhead behind it at address. Result: The outside-in swing becomes even more pronounced.

One footnote to alignment is the positioning of the feet and the difference between being open or closed and aiming left or right. Remember, when you are in a correct square starting position, the line across the toes of both feet is parallel to the target line. Opening the stance involves moving one foot, the left, back from this line a few inches. The right foot does not move. Aiming left involves moving *both* feet. The left moves back and the right moves forward. The same applies in reverse for closing the stance versus aiming right. The reason I mention this is that I see many people who, in an effort to minimize their slice for example, begin aiming too far right when attempting to close the stance. They are moving both feet, not just one. As a result, the mind's eye sees the target well left of where the body is aiming, and an over-the-top slicing downswing occurs anyway.

This practice station will help you establish good alignment habits.

One way to check your alignment is to place clubs down on the ground, one representing the target line, another for the line of the feet. Then, after assuming the address position, have a friend or spouse take a third club and hold it against your knees, hips, forearms, shoulders, and eye line. You may feel contorted when you get these lines all parallel if you have been doing something else, but keep working on it.

Mirror work is an excellent way to practice the correct setup as well. You will find your body very quickly gets used to being in the square position. Plus, you will find this address invaluable in assisting your efforts to make your best swing.

CHAPTER 7

Ten More Yards

I strongly believe that most amateur golfers suffer more from mishit and misdirected shots than from lack of distance. Therefore, I am somewhat amused at the level of concern club and ball manufacturers, and the golfing public, place on greater and greater distance. Many golfers fail to realize that the swing inefficiencies that cause shots to be mishit and/or misdirected also cause a severe loss of distance; that if the swing corrections necessary to hit the ball more solidly and/or straighter are made, increased distance will be a natural byproduct. I think it's important to mention here that other factors also contribute to loss of distance when shots are constantly being mishit or misdirected. One such factor is the golfer's loss of confidence, which can most readily be observed in tentativeness in the swing. A certain flow, a certain rhythm is obviously missing, as opposed to the swing that is made with confidence and is, therefore, characterized by a controlled aggressiveness.

Other distance robbers that can result from mishit and/or misdirected shots are tension and excessive grip pressure, natural offshoots of poorly

Greg Norman and Tiger Woods swing confidently, with controlled aggression. Also, like so many top pros, they know that added distance is a byproduct of a sound setup and swing.

hit shots. You are probably familiar with the phenomenon of trying to "steer" the ball. You may also be familiar with excessive body and grip tension, resulting in a shorter, quicker swing than you might otherwise make.

Such ancillary problems can occur simply because of loss of confidence, which, in turn, is the result of swing deficiencies that produce poor shots. It is best, therefore, to focus on the deficiencies that cause the poorly hit or errant shot and not to be concerned with the too infrequent good hit that doesn't go as far as one might like.

That being said, certainly there is a percentage of golfers who do not hit the ball far enough to enjoy the game (or at least not as far as they are capable) but who also hit the ball straight enough and solid enough

Faulty positions—in the takeaway (top left), *at the top of the backswing* (top right), *and on the downswing* (bottom left)—*cause poor impact positions* (bottom right), *draining power from the swing and misdirecting shots.*

on a fairly consistent basis. These players include, but are not limited to, senior men who are losing flexibility and to some degree strength; women who may be lacking strength in legs, arms, wrists, hands, and fingers; and others who simply exhibit swing characteristics that adversely affect distance.

Other than the influence of the club, ball, and physical characteristics of the golfer, distance is a function of two things: solid contact between club and ball and clubhead speed at impact. Solid contact is a function of a good setup and a swing that is on plane with proper support of the body movement—in other words, all the things we have been looking at in the previous chapters. Clubhead speed at impact is a function of the length of a clubhead's *controlled* arc, the width of a clubhead's controlled arc, the speed with which the body moves through its required positions in the downswing, the arm swing speed in the downswing, and the cocking and properly timed uncocking of the wrists.

Length of arc simply refers to the length of one's backswing—more precisely the distance the clubhead has traveled when it reaches its farthest position in the backswing. You will notice I included the word *controlled* with length of arc. This is because simply taking the club farther back does not mean you will hit the ball farther. In fact, you may hit it shorter if you compromise certain swing principles to do so. For example, getting the clubhead to go farther back by loosening the grip at the top of the backswing or by collapsing the left arm at the top or by overturning the shoulders and/or hips because the left heel has been lifted excessively off the ground will not result in greater clubhead speed at impact.

Ideally, I want you to blend sufficient length of backswing with control and maximum body torque. This means the shaft of the club should be approximately parallel to the ground at the top with the shoulders turned 90 degrees; but with the lower body (hips) resisting this turn.

If a person's backswing is too short, the reason will involve one or more of these components: (1) amount of shoulder turn, (2) length of arm swing, and (3) amount of wrist cock. Lack of shoulder turn can result from loss of flexibility; lifting the arms too vertically in the backswing; or possibly having the chin too low in the address position, which prevents the left shoulder from moving completely back. Also, as previously mentioned, overall body tension can prevent the complete turn.

Employing a 90 degree shoulder turn, creating a wide swing arc, and setting the club in the full parallel position are all vital links to power. Letting the lower body resist, as the upper body coils, helps build powerful torque.

Arm swing length that is not sufficient is often owing to lack of flexibility in the upper left arm and shoulder area. In addition, like the shoulder turn, it can be hampered by excessive tension or overcontrol of the swing. Another factor that can contribute to the overly short arm swing is a backswing that is too quick. Quick and short go together in golf and are not a good combination. Although quick usually is the result of being short, it is a relationship that you should be aware of. A good exercise to enhance flexibility and become more aware of the optimum length of arm swing back is the Flexibility Drill I recommended in Chapter 1.

Recognize it is possible to have a full 90 degree shoulder turn without a sufficient length of arm swing. In such a case, as with an insufficient turn, you will not feel powerful at the end of your backswing, and your instincts will tell you to force the club down, to try to create speed artificially in the downswing to make up for the backswing deficiencies. Another incorrect scenario that is not uncommon is the left arm that bends excessively because the shoulders fail to turn fully. It is precisely at that moment in the backswing when the shoulders (which should continue to turn) stop, that the left arm starts to bend. I often refer to such an interaction as *substitution of motion*. Since the straight left arm can't get the club back all the way owing to the failure of the shoulder turn, it bends excessively to get the club back farther. The club may end up far enough back, but control of the club is sacrificed for length of arc. The same thing occurs if the shoulders overturn, or the shoulders turn the correct amount and the arms swing back too far, with or without excessive left elbow bend. In all these cases, control of the club is compromised, resulting in a downswing that will be out of sequence or just plain out of position.

The third mechanical component that influences length of backswing arc is the cocking of the wrists—the hinging that should occur naturally in the backswing at the base of the thumbs. Hinging can be interfered with by an incorrect placement of the hands on the club, particularly an excessively strong grip; grip pressure that is so tight the wrists become rigid; a backswing that is so flat the clubhead is not ascending sufficiently enough to cause the wrists to naturally hinge.

Occasionally, I see a female student who has been chastised by a male playing partner—often her husband!—for overswinging, totally eliminate wrist hinge in the backswing to correct the problem. This is a classic example of fixing a problem incorrectly, because the overswing is almost always the result of a left arm that collapses or a loosening of the grip, not a wrist hinge fault. Eliminating the hinging and thus the correct unhinging in the downswing is like jumping from the frying pan into the fire. The wrist hinge is an absolute necessity in the golf swing for power and for its positive influence on the plane of the swing.

An excellent drill to review the correct hinging action in the backswing is called the *Vertical Hinge Drill*. Take your address position in front of a mirror. Without changing the posture established by the club you are using, hinge your wrists vertically upward so the shaft is moving toward your nose. Be careful not to bend your arms as you do this. When the hinge is completed, you will have approximately a 90 degree angle between your left arm and clubshaft. Now, holding this position, turn your shoulders 90 degrees. The resulting position is where you should be halfway back in a backswing that has incorporated the correct hinging of the wrists. Repeat this drill motion several times, then make a conventional backswing to this halfway-back point and see if you can assume the same position as when doing the drill.

It is important to recognize that professionals who have excellent golf swings may not all cock their wrists fully at the same point in the backswing. Some hinge their wrists early, some late. However, *all* hinge their wrists fully and hold the hinge until the proper moment in the downswing.

This takes us to the concept of the properly timed release of the wrist cock in the downswing. Even though the wrist hinge in the backswing may be executed correctly, one cannot assume the same will be true for the unhinging down. In fact, improper unhinging is quite a universal problem among amateur players. Why? I think the hit impulse we discussed in Chapter 1 is partly to blame. The dominance of the stronger right hand over the weaker left (as is usually the case with right-handed players) is also involved. An incorrect perception about how to create power in a swing—which destroys correct sequence of motion in the downswing and will be discussed later in this chapter—is also an integral factor. To some extent, strength is involved as well. Regardless of the reason, early unhinging, "casting" the clubhead, the premature uncocking of the wrists, is the result. More than 50 percent of your potential clubhead speed can be spent before you arrive at impact. The loss of distance will be accompanied by many fat or thin shots as well, as the club reaches the bottom of its arc before it gets to the ball when the unhinging is premature. In such an event, you not only lose clubhead speed but also experience loss of distance because of the unsolid contact between club and ball.

A very good drill that addresses this problem is called the *1-2-3 Drill.* You can combine it with the Vertical Hinge Drill or you can swing back to a halfway-back position, as previously described. In this drill, you rehearse the correct initiation of the downswing motion on 1 and on 2, then release into a complete motion down and through on 3. As you rehearse the downward motion on 1 and 2, the goal is to subtly slide your hips targetward, as you simultaneously allow your arms to fall *without* any change in wrist position. After you rehearse 1, simply return to the backswing position from which you started and repeat the rehearsal for a second time. Return again to the backswing position and now allow the downswing and partial through swing to occur as you execute 3. You are rehearsing proper sequence of motion in a downswing, you are feeling a delayed uncocking of your wrists, and you are sensing the clubhead approaching the ball from inside the target line. Primarily, however, you are sensing the correct unhinging of the wrists at the proper moment in the downswing. This is a sensation you want to eventually incorporate into a full swing when additional force is applied.

The width of a clubhead's controlled arc is another component to clubhead speed at impact. Theoretically, the wider the radius of your swing's circle, the more clubhead speed can be generated as it swings along that circle.

That is why some players, such as Jack Nicklaus, Greg Norman, Davis Love III, and Tiger Woods, have a later wrist cock in their backswings. They are consciously extending their left hands and arms as much as

Like so many long ball hitters, Greg Norman delays the hinging action of the wrists in the backswing to create a wide swing arc. He has the strength required to do this. The average player is better off allowing the hinging process to be farther along at this point in the backswing.

possible in their backswing. However, although late, they do eventually fully cock their wrists, and they do swing the club back correctly on plane. Some amateur players attempt to emulate the wide takeaway and backswing by incorrectly moving the club, hands, and arms out and above the plane in the takeaway and/or fail to sufficiently cock the wrists during the completion of the backswing. I would rather the recreational golfer be more concerned with nice width and extension of the left arm (but not rigid) at the top of the backswing and then be extremely focused on extension of the left arm at impact and postimpact, where so many swings show far too much collapsing. The Simulated Impact Drill, discussed in Chapter 2, is excellent for working on this.

If you sense you are not extended enough in the takeaway—for example, if you are guilty of taking the club back too far to the inside—by all means work on a straighter, more extended takeaway. But be aware this can be done to a fault. Remember, when you reach Position 1 (Chapter 3), the right arm is *not* extended like the left but rather slightly folded at the elbow.

The next factor to look at that influences clubhead speed is the speed with which the body moves in the downswing. Such a component of the swing cannot be discussed, however, without concurrent discussion of arm swing speed. You do not, for example, want to speed up the movement of the knees, legs, and hips in the downswing and leave the arms and club too far behind. Yes, there is a relationship between the speed with which you move your body and the speed with which your arms swing—but that relationship is not one to one. Tiger Woods is a wonderful example to look at. His prodigious distance, to a large degree, comes from the speed with which he moves his hips and legs in the downswing. However, he also has the strength and athletic ability to swing his arms at a very fast rate. His hips provide the lead, and the arms follow that lead, but the arm speed is not totally a product of the action of the lower body.

If you were able, in other words, to move your hips as fast as Woods does in the downswing, it would be very unlikely your arm swing would be able to keep up, that the increase in your arm swing speed would exponentially keep up with the increase in the speed of the hip motion. In fact, the same would be true for most tour players. As skilled and adept as they already are in executing a golf swing mechanically correctly, *if* they were able to move the lower body as fast as Woods does (and still maintain control and balance), even they would find it difficult, if not impossible, to swing their arms as fast as he does.

That does not mean, however, you do not want to speed up a lower body that is moving too slowly, so that you take advantage of the arm speed with which you are capable of producing. I caution you, however, that the arms should swing only as fast as the body is able to support, and the body should move only as fast as the arms are able to keep up, which means I have to rely on the student's own sensations to tell him or her when enough is enough. So I broach this subject cautiously, as it deals with the element of timing, which is difficult to express in words.

To some extent, you must recognize that the ability to produce arm and body speed in the downswing is based on physical attributes. However, the major mechanical problem that diminishes the potential for

To generate clubhead speed on the downswing, the arms should swing only as fast as the body is able to support, and the body should move only as fast as the arms are able to keep up.

speed for many golfers is in the right leg action in the backswing. For the hips and legs to spring forward with natural speed and power at the initiation of the downswing, the right leg must act as a brace, a stable post if you will, as you swing back. This means the right knee *must* remain flexed the same amount it was flexed at address. It also must not move laterally away from the target, so that the weight moves to the outside of the right foot. This happens far too frequently; when it happens, you have lost all hope of starting the downswing correctly in proper sequence and starting it with sufficient speed of the lower body.

If your leg is straightening, it may be the result of lack of strength. If that is the case, I urge you to do some simple strengthening exercises such as knee bends or squats, riding a stationary bike, or simply standing on the right leg only and bending the knee for twenty to thirty seconds.

On the other hand, your leg may be straightening simply because you are not paying enough attention to the importance of keeping it flexed and braced. Swing a few times in front of a mirror and check this. Correct it immediately if you detect a problem.

The final aspect of hitting the golf ball farther deals with more subjective elements in the swing. As you involve yourself with some of the swing's mechanical components, you must not overlook the lubricant that allows them to mesh correctly in a properly coordinated motion. This consists of the rhythm and tempo of the motion and how they affect your ability to sequence and time the components correctly so you get the most power out of your swing. Certainly, I have touched on this in regard to the arm swing speed as it relates to the body motion speed and in regard to the uncocking of the wrists. At this point I would like to be more specific.

For many golfers the irony of experiencing success in hitting the ball farther is in not trying to do so. This is because their expenditure of effort is excessive—the issue is overly forced. It is precisely this active attempt to hit the ball harder than you should that makes the swing break down. Conversely, all of us have experienced that swing when, in a conscious effort to slow things down, we hit a career shot that goes a far greater distance than we ever would have imagined. This is because even if your swing incorporates mechanical flaws they can be greatly diminished if you swing more slowly in both directions, back and down.

Moreover, some swing flaws actually disappear altogether when you swing more smoothly, fluidly, and slowly. This may be an interesting concept for those of you who are constantly tinkering with the mechanics of your swing, when in fact your flaws may be 100 percent attributable to its tempo.

For any swing to be good, there needs to be a well-coordinated relationship between the motion of the body, the swinging of the arms, and the hinging/unhinging of the wrists. You must swing at whatever rate of speed is necessary for this coordinated effort to occur. For most, it is slower rather than faster. I find myself constantly using the analogy of the Model T Ford going eighty miles per hour on the Interstate. It won't be long before the car starts to break apart; it's not designed for that speed. As your swing mechanics improve (Model T to 1955 Chevy to 1978 Buick to 1998 Lincoln Mark VIII), you can gradually increase your speed of motion. But if you are trying to swing faster than your mechanical ability allows, you will most definitely have a breakdown.

No specific areas of the swing are more important for the well-coordinated effort than the takeaway and the change of direction at the top of the backswing. It's possible to swing too slowly, such that athleticism and fluidity of motion are lost. However, more prevalent is the swing that is too fast, quick, or jerky. When I see a swing begin this way, my reaction is that the golfer does not have the correct perception of how clubhead speed is created in the downswing. It builds gradually, from the ground up, allowing the involvement of all the sources of power in the swing.

The smooth, slow takeaway becomes important because it encourages a mutual concurrent involvement of arms, body, and club, allowing the clubhead to move back in a controlled, correct direction and promoting a full coil at the completion of the backswing. Too fast a takeaway is often done with such quick arm movement that the body gets left behind—it doesn't have time to respond. The shoulders and hips don't turn sufficiently; the body weight does not move fully into the right side. The result, usually, is that the club moves back on an excessively steep plane, leading to an outside-in downswing. Another possibility is the fast takeaway accompanied by a fast rotational motion of the body. The hips and shoulders turn too much too soon, pulling the club off-plane to the inside. Body weight is forced onto the front leg and the

Having the lower body trigger the downswing is a key move in the change of direction of the arms and club and promotes an on-plane downswing.

downswing can be either too inside-out or outside-in, but rarely on plane.

The other critical area of the swing that requires much more attention than most people give it is the change of direction at the top—the transition. It is in this area that the better player has a distinctly different perception and execution of the motion.

For the club and arms to correctly descend on plane, to drop into the slot, so the clubhead can approach the ball properly from the inside and so the uncocking of the wrists can be delayed, it is imperative the downswing begin with the lower body. This means that as the arms and club ascend to the completion of the backswing, the lower left side of the body starts moving forward. If the left heel is off the ground, it must return to the ground immediately as the left knee and hip move laterally toward the target. This forward movement of the lower body is actually what slows the upward movement of the club and arms and ultimately causes their change of direction. The expert swinger allows this to happen. He or she knows it is an active lower body and a passive upper body that causes the optimum club movement. The poorer swinger does just the opposite: The upper body is active; the lower body is passive. This is one example of improper sequence of motion. The precision required for correct sequencing cannot possibly occur if the arm swing is quick and forceful, moving too fast to allow the interceding movement of the lower body to lead the club and arms down. Without this correct sequencing, everything bad that can happen in a downswing will happen. Body weight will not transfer forward. The club is thrown off-plane. The wrists will uncock early. All power is lost, along with accurate, solid contact.

As the lower body leads, the club falls nicely onto the original shaft angle plane.

The initial passivity of the upper body in the correct downswing applies to the hands, arms, shoulders, and wrists. They all fall downward in response to the lower body. Regarding the wrists and the timing of their uncocking, we again see a major difference between the good and the not-so-good swing. In the good swing, the wrists are a natural link, a free hinge at the beginning of the downswing. Good swingers apply no force at the hinge at this point. They wait. The hinge stays intact until the downswing movement of the arms is sufficient enough that centrifugal force causes the wrists to begin unhinging on their own. It is precisely here that expert swingers then apply additional force of their own to allow for maximum clubhead speed at the ball. In the incorrect motion, the golfer succumbs to the hit instinct, often enhanced by the overly fast swing, and applies this force of the wrists early—as soon as the downswing begins. Result: Maximum clubhead speed is

Continuation of the motion.

reached well before it reaches the golf ball, and the golfer experiences severe loss of distance.

The lesson to be learned here is that distance is a factor of several things, some mechanical, some more subjective. Work on your distance mechanics, but do so only within the parameters of a swing that is of proper speed and rhythm, so that correct sequence of motion and proper timing of the wrists can be incorporated into the mix. Start the club back slowly, be patient as you complete the backswing, start down with slow arm speed initially as the lower body transfers weight to the forward leg, and then think of creating your maximum clubhead speed, past the ball—not at it and certainly not before it.

CHAPTER 8

Swing Faults, Causes, Corrections, Pitfalls

This chapter identifies some of the most common swing faults, their causes, and corrective procedures, along with drills designed to help eliminate them. I have also included common pitfalls students should be aware of as they execute drills and go through the process of improving their golf swings.

1. Swing Fault: Clubhead too inside on the takeaway
2. Swing Fault: Reverse weight shift in the backswing
3. Swing Fault: Poor top of backswing position: too steep and/or too long
4. Swing Fault: Improper wrist action throughout the swing, including early release
5. Swing Fault: Backswing too short
6. Swing Fault: Club is over the top, outside-in in the downswing
7. Fault: Inside-out downswing

1. Swing Fault: Club too Inside on the Takeaway

If the club is too inside on the takeaway, the result will be either a loop to the outside down, causing pulls and slices, or a downswing that is too inside-out causing pushes and hooks.

Cause #1: The clubface is fanning open in the takeaway owing to a grip that is too weak or because the golfer is attempting to rotate the face into a toe-up position at Position 1.

Correction: Strengthen the grip and *feel* the clubface aiming downward as you make a conscious effort to take the club back straighter. The right arm should stay above the left longer in the takeaway than previously, and you should feel more extension of the arms initially in the backswing.

Drill #1: Put a ball on a tee about eight inches behind the ball you are hitting, then knock it off the tee backward as you execute your backswing.

When trying to rotate the face into a toe-up position, some players take the club back too far inside the target line.

Drill #2: Swing back, trying to get the hosel of your club to touch the inside portion of a shaft stuck into the ground about a yard to the right of the ball of your right foot.

Cause #2: The clubhead is moving too inside on the takeaway (with the face either fanning open or not) because the hands are separating *out,* away from the body, as they start back.

Correction: As you move your hands back in the takeaway, you must feel as if they are going to hit your right leg. As you do this, allow your wrists to begin hinging sooner so the clubhead ascends more quickly, allowing it to stay outside your hands until you reach Position 1.

Drill #1: After assuming your address position, have a friend stand just to your left and hold a clubshaft horizontal to the ground and against your right hand. Practice your takeaway without pushing the horizontal shaft outward.

Drill #2: Another drill, which can be done at home with an old

Here, I am practicing Drill #2, to correct an overly inside takeaway action.

table, is to take your address position, with your hands against the table edge and the clubhead underneath it. The table edge will prevent your hands from moving out in the takeaway. Notice that as the hands move back, they will gradually move *inward,* which is correct. As the hands move back, begin cocking your wrists so the clubhead will hit the under side of the tabletop, instead of escaping out from underneath it, as it ascends upward. This will give you the proper feel of a correct takeaway.

Pitfall: For each of these inside takeaways and accompanying corrective drills, be careful not to get too stiff in your arms and wrists and also be very careful not to tilt your upper body left (targetward) as you take the club back. This is a very common fault when making this takeaway correction and will result in a reverse weight shift. Work on your takeaway facing a mirror to check this and prevent it from happening.

A second pitfall is to separate your hands and arms *away* from your body in the takeaway in your effort to stop the club from going too inside.

Swing Fault 2: the player employs a faulty reverse pivot action on the backswing.

Just remember it's the clubhead you are trying to keep farther out, not your hands or arms. The operative phrase is hands *in* clubhead *out*.

2. Swing Fault: Reverse Weight Shift in the Backswing

As demonstrated in the photo at the left, the weight is shifting in a reverse direction in the backswing, and the arm swing is taking the club back either on, above, or under the correct plane in the takeaway.

Cause: The head and left shoulder are dropping downward, rather than moving back level. This can result from an overzealous effort to "Keep the head down," an incorrect effort not to sway, a left knee that is bending excessively downward in the takeaway, and/or a right hip and leg that are sliding to the right, away from the target.

Correction: Turn your shoulders 90 degrees, moving the left shoulder over the inside right knee area. Keep your right knee flexed and braced, moving weight to the inside of the right foot.

Drill: Use a light chair, such as a plastic lawn chair, against your right hip and leg to monitor lower body motion. Swing back,

Doing this drill and turning your shoulders rather than tilting them (or letting the head and left shoulder dip downward) will help you cure your reverse pivot problem. The chair will discourage your right hip and leg from sliding laterally, away from the target, another cause of the reverse weight shift.

keeping your right knee flexed. As your hips begin to turn, do not let your right hip drift to the right so that it pushes the chair up. As your shoulders turn, you will notice your head moving slightly to the right, which is correct. When you have correctly completed your turn, your shoulders will have turned 90 degrees; your head and left shoulder will be over a point just inside your right knee and your back line will be angled away from the target. Keep doing this over and over until it starts to feel natural. Your feeling will be that your head is moving much more to the right than it actually is. Repetition is the key to imprinting this new move into your swing. As you practice this motion, occasionally do it with your eyes closed and focus on the feeling of what you are doing.

Pitfall: If your club previously had been moving back on plane with faulty body motion, in all likelihood it will now move back too far inside. This is because your shoulders are turning more level and more correctly. If this happens, your overall backswing will get too flat, resulting in a too inside or an outside-in downswing. Remember, your goal here is to have your shaft parallel to your stance line when it ascends to a horizontal to the ground position. If your takeaway previously had been above the plane, your new body motion should put it nicely on plane. If your takeaway previously had been too inside, which is quite likely, allowing your arms to extend more than they have been will help move your upper body more right as your shoulders turn back.

3. Swing Fault: Poor Top of Backswing Position: Too Steep and/or Too Long

The result of these incorrect top of backswing positions will usually be an over-the-top downswing with a premature uncocking of the wrists. *Over the top* is synonymous with *outside-in,* so pulls and slices can be expected. With the premature uncocking, loss of power and thin and fat shots will result.

Cause: The left arm has swung back to a too vertical position at the completion of the backswing. Most often this is the result of a too inside takeaway that triggers the compensatory vertical lift to the top. The vertical left arm can then bend excessively, causing the overswing. The same top-of-backswing position can also occur, from a too steep back-

This is an overly long and overly steep position at the top. You will not be able to recover from this position with any degree of consistency.

swing all the way from the address. In either case, the right elbow will also be too high at the top of the backswing.

Correction: The key here is to simply hold the top of backswing to a shorter position after making a correct takeaway. Most golfers who overswing or get too vertical back cannot believe how short back they must feel to keep the club in position, so don't be afraid to exaggerate the correction.

Drill: Put a headcover under your right elbow at address and make some backswings; do not let the elbow move away from your side, causing the headcover to fall to the ground. Keep your left arm straight and turn your shoulders 90 degrees as you do this. Hit some balls this way. It's okay to drop the headcover in the follow-through but not in the backswing. Even though you will feel powerless at first, which will make you want to rush the downswing, it is a false feeling. Resist the urge to force the club down; instead swing smoothly and slowly. Understand that this top-of-backswing position with the headcover under your arm is an exaggerated position. But this is precisely what must be done in practice to effect change. As you become accustomed to the exaggerated position, you soon will reach the point at which you can afford to swing back without the headcover and trust that the right elbow will not move excessively far away from your side. This ideal right arm position is what I refer to as the *tray position,* or the position a waiter's arm would be in when supporting a large tray. The upper right arm would be parallel to the ground at the top of the backswing, no higher.

Pitfall: You must be careful here not to fail to turn your shoulders 90 degrees in the backswing. The problem we are dealing with is an overly

Keeping a headcover under your right elbow and your left arm relatively straight as you swing back will help you correct the top of backswing problems depicted in the photo on the previous page.

vertical and long arm swing. You do not want to compromise the full shoulder turn in your effort to get shorter and flatter in the backswing. Also, be careful not to start taking the club back too inside in the take-away. Even though your right arm is somewhat restricted, it does not mean you cannot move the clubhead back nicely on plane.

4. Swing Fault: Improper Wrist Action Throughout the Swing, Including Early Release

Common swing faults involving the wrists include the following: The wrists are not hinging correctly or soon enough in the backswing (which often results in an overswing), they are uncocking too soon in the downswing, and they fail to rehinge correctly or soon enough in the through swing.

Cause: Backswing wrist cock problems are caused by an improper grip that interferes with the natural hinging process, a backswing take-away that is too flat, and/or grip pressure that is way too excessive. In regard to the latter, I find that almost without exception, all golfers, male and female alike, grip the club much tighter than they should.

This cuppy through swing wrist position signals possible incorrect wrist action on the backswing and reveals that the right hand applied force prematurely in the downswing.

Unhinging too soon in the downswing is caused by a prematurely active right hand. It forces the wrists to release early and is an instinctive problem that all golfers must deal with. It involves what we refer to as timing. These back and downswing wrist action swing faults often result in dead wrists in the through swing, interfering with the natural rehinging process that should occur in this segment of the swing.

Correction: Loosen your grip pressure until you feel you are not controlling the club but that the club is controlling your wrists. Allow your wrists to hinge at the base of the thumbs as you swing a club halfway back and halfway through. If you do this in front of a mirror, notice the angle created between arm and clubshaft when the hinge is complete, either in the backswing or through swing. This angle should be 90 degrees. At this point, you should feel your wrists acting as a free link, responding to the movement and weight of the club.

Drill #1: Insert a golf tee into the butt end of the grip, preferably on a 5, 6, or 7 iron. The tee is used as a pointer. At the end of a half-backswing (left arm approximately parallel to the ground) and at the end of a half–through swing (right arm approximately parallel to the ground), monitor the position of the club by observing where the tee is pointing at these points in the swing. If the wrists are properly hinged with the shaft on plane, the tee will be pointing to the ground, slightly inside the target line in the backswing position and to the target line in the follow-through position. Both points will be about three feet from the ball you are addressing. After you hinge your wrists back, pause for a moment to see where the tee is pointing. If your position is correct, swing your arms down holding your wrist hinge as long as you possibly can. Don't worry. Centrifugal force will cause you to uncock your wrists. Your job is to retain the hinge until that natural occurrence takes place. Once it does, swing your arms forward with extension of the right arm and recock your wrists fully so the tee again points to the ground to the target line. Hit balls as you do this drill, preferably teed up. Swing smoothly and at half speed. This action can gradually be blended into a fuller golf swing as you become more adept in its execution. When so done, your swing will be more on plane, your contact with the ball will be more solid and consistent, and you will feel much more power with much less effort.

This drill, done with a tee inserted in the butt end of the club, will help you correct faulty wrist action. If the wrists are properly hinged and the shaft is on plane, the tee will point slightly inside the target line on the backswing (left) *and at the target line in the follow-through position* (right).

Drill #2: Another drill procedure you can do focuses just on wrist cock retention down. I refer to it as a progression drill, because you execute it with different right hand positions on the club. You begin with the right hand significantly separated from the left, then gradually move it closer as you perfect each step.

At the first stage of this progression drill, you begin by holding the club with your normal left hand grip, the right hand off the club. Bring the shaft up to horizontal to the ground, and rest the shaft into the middle of the fingers of your open right hand. Your right hand should be well down the shaft, about eighteen inches from the left. From here, swing your arms back just a few inches. As you do so, use the fingers of your right hand to apply upward pressure on the shaft. Your left arm should remain straight. You now rehearse a partial downswing by concurrently shifting your weight forward and allowing your arms to descend in response. As they do so, use the open fingers of the right hand to *hold the shaft up.* When you uncock your wrists prematurely in the downswing, your right hand is applying *downward* pressure on the shaft before it should. You want to use the right hand to apply power, but you must be patient and wait until the body, arms, and club have moved into the correct position.

In this drill, you are training the right hand to do exactly the opposite of what it wants to do. You are making the right hand hold the shaft up. After making the first rehearsal downswing, go back to the backswing position from which you started and rehearse the downswing move again. When you finish the downswing rehearsal correctly, your hands will be directly in front of your body and your right hand will be holding the shaft up to a parallel-to-the ground position. Go back to the backswing position one more time and start the downswing again. Only this time, no rehearsal—no stopping. Allow the swing to continue all the way to a complete finish. You must, however, continue to use your right hand to hold the shaft from releasing until the hand swings down and forward to a point directly in front of your body. Now let the shaft slide off your open fingers as you release it from the right hand. Put a tee in the ground and clip it as you swing through. You are just now beginning to feel what a correctly timed release is.

The next step is to move the right hand up the shaft, a little closer to the left. The little finger of the right hand should be on the shaft, just off the club's grip, but adjacent to the grip's end. Do the same procedure as before: two rehearsal downswings, then let the club slide out of the open right hand. Use the right hand to hold the shaft up in the two rehearsal downswings. Relate to the feel of this motion.

The final step is to move your right hand onto the grip next to your left, but keep all five fingers on the grip. In essence, this is a ten-fingered grip with a *slight* separation of the hands. Your right hand is no longer open; your right hand fingers surround the grip normally. You start this practice swing from a conventional address position and execute the drill procedure just as before—two rehearsal downswings, all the way through on the third. Even though you do not let the club slide out of your right hand at this stage of the drill, you continue to use it to hold the shaft up for as long as possible as you swing your arms down. Retain the same feeling you had before in the other two stages. Do not worry that the club will release too late, or not catch up. It will. This is what is so difficult to discern.

Your sensations tell you the clubhead will never catch up. That's why some players want to help it by releasing early; but don't discount the influence of centrifugal force in the mix. It not only triggers the release point but also assists the movement of the club to quickly catch up to the hands and arms at or just after impact. It is a facet of the swing that you must learn to trust, and it is one of the major elements of the golf swing that separates the good player from the less skilled.

Pitfall: Remember that the hinging, unhinging, and rehinging of the wrists in the golf swing are components of the full swing motion that must be blended and timed with the swinging of the arms and the movement of the body. A problem will arise if you get so involved with the hinging/unhinging process that you forget, for example, that you must swing the arms all the way back and you must turn your shoulders as you do so. I will see on occasion a student who neglects these aspects of the swing when working on the wrists, and the backswing then becomes too short and too upright.

5. Swing Fault: Backswing too Short Owing to Incomplete Shoulder Turn and too Short an Arm Swing

When the backswing is too short because of an incomplete shoulder turn, the left arm often bends excessively as a result. This leads to an excessively forced downswing to try to make up for lost power, most often resulting in an outside-in swing path.

Cause: Misperceptions, inflexibility, and a drifting right hip and leg will prevent the shoulders from turning completely. For the latter problem, please review Swing Fault 2. A common misperception in the execution of a backswing is that if your left shoulder turns back into your chin, you

Keeping the chin down and locked in position can discourage a full shoulder turn and result in a backswing that is too short. If the chin is down and rigid it can result in a backswing that doesn't go any farther back than this.

will have turned sufficiently. However, that depends on where your chin is. If you move your chin down and/or forward as you turn your left shoulder back, by the time they meet, the left shoulder will most definitely not have turned a full 90 degrees. In addition, as the left shoulder moves back and contacts a correctly positioned chin, the chin should be pushed back a little by the continuing backward motion of the shoulder. The other option is for the chin to hold its position and block any further shoulder movement, resulting in a less than 90 degree turn. Another correct scenario for the backswing shoulder motion is for the head to be moving slightly to the right as the shoulders begin to turn back. If this occurs, the left shoulder will make its first contact with the chin only when it has completed its proper turn, because the chin has moved slightly right during the backswing with the head.

Inflexibility is another major cause of the too short backswing. Please refer to Chapter 1, which details the wonderful Flexibility Drill for the shoulders, upper torso, and left arm. Remember, keeping the left arm straight enhances your turn. As soon as it bends, the shoulders stop turning.

Drill: Place a shaft across your shoulders and hold it there with your hands crossed, left on right shoulder and right on left. Work on turning your shoulders 90 degrees as you observe yourself in a mirror. The shaft across your shoulders helps you determine when you have gone the full 90 degrees. When done correctly, your left shoulder will be over a point just inside your right knee.

Pitfall: The caution here is not to overturn your body back. If you lift your left heel excessively and allow your hips to overturn, you will turn your shoulders too much as well. Remember too that the arms swing the club *up* as the shoulders turn; they do not follow the turn of the

Hold a shaft across your shoulders as you make your backswing turn to help you determine when you have gone the full 90 degrees. Notice how my chin and head swiveled to accommodate the full winding action of the shoulders.

body and swing the club too flat and around behind you. As you work on turning more, this is a very easy mistake to make.

6. Swing Fault: Club Is Over the Top, Outside-In in the Downswing

If your divots are too deep, and usually deeper toward the toe side, your club is probably over the top, outside-in in the downswing. You feel handcuffed at impact, unable to get the club through. The ball is often pulled left with shorter clubs, but with the longer ones the ball may start left and slice too far right. Or the ball may simply go right immediately. Thin shots, tops, and an occasional fat shot are also in the mix along with shanks and pop-ups with the driver when the action becomes pronounced.

Cause: A great deal of this book has been devoted to the many reasons this type of downswing is so prevalent. The hit instinct, the fact the ball is on the ground while you swing the club up in the air, a more

This type of follow-through indicates that the right shoulder, right hand, and club all moved out, over the correct plane on the downswing. I may be looking left here, but that's only because the ball started flying in that direction, before slicing.

physically dominant right side of the body, improper tempo, and a grip that is too weak all enter into the mix. However, when all is said and done, the physical action that moves the club out above the plane in the downswing is an incorrectly overactive upper right side of the body. This includes a right hand that uncocks the wrists prematurely, which most often results in an outward movement of the club. This also includes a right arm and hand that push the club out as it moves down without necessarily forcing the wrists to uncock. And, finally, this also includes an upper right torso and shoulder area that moves out rather than more downward as the downswing begins. We also have to consider the faulty action of a left hip that does not move laterally enough toward the target at the outset of the downswing; rather, it spins left, promoting the upper right side to perform any or all the incorrect movements just listed. In Chapter 7 we discussed the importance of initiating the downswing with the lower body and the relationship of arm speed and tempo to one's success in being able to accomplish this.

Correction: Obviously, we must train the upper right side to become more passive as the downswing is initiated, allowing the club and arms to fall more *downward* than *outward.* Starting down slowly with the wrist cock retained will help, as will initiating the movement down with the lower body. However, these motions are easier said than done. Drills *must* be implemented to make the body and arms perform more correctly. Knowing what you should do will not effect change. We must physically make the body do it through training.

Drill #1: One particular swing shape I see often, much more than any other, is a backswing that is too flat but that then lifts too vertically as the top is reached. As a natural continuation of the motion, the club then comes out in the downswing. I call it an *in, up, and over.* To counter such an action, I often use a *Reverse Loop Drill.* I have the golfer execute an exactly opposite swing, which can be identified by the phrase *out, up, and under.* Often, to make a correction you must exaggerate to the extent you try to do exactly the opposite of what you were doing wrong. This is the intent of this drill. It is of interest to note that when students attempt to execute such a swing, as much as they feel they are making the out, up, and under loop, I often see a swing that is basically correctly on plane, both up and down.

In executing this motion, start the club back to the *outside* even if your arms initially move away from your body a little. Then feel your arms and club swinging *up*. As you reach the end of the backswing, feel your hands and club moving decidedly *behind* you as they swing down. If done correctly, you will have the distinct sensation of swinging out to right field postimpact. Allow this to happen as your body rotates to a finish. It helps to angle a shaft in the ground to your right, midway between your stance and target lines. Use the end of the shaft as a visual reference for your swing. You want the clubhead to ascend on its outside and descend on its inside.

Pitfall: Often a student will start the club back correctly to the outside, but then instead of swinging the club up to the top before dropping it to the inside as he or she starts down, the student will swing the club back around the body, too flat. This is not an out and up backswing; it's an out and around. If this happens, the downswing plane becomes too flat, and it's difficult to make solid contact with the ball. Also, recognize that this is an extreme arm swing drill. It is done only temporarily to give you the sensation of the reverse loop.

Over time the extreme sensations you first feel will diminish; and though you may be making exactly the same motion, you won't sense it. Consequently, you may try to make the loop even bigger to regain the sensations you first experienced. This, of course, is wrong. In fact, as time goes by, you actually want to temper the reverse loop action, if in fact you succeeded in doing it in the first place. Swinging back on a plane that is slightly more upright than the downswing plane is technically correct, and many professionals do this. If you retain this swing characteristic, you will be in good shape. Just make sure the loop to the inside does not become excessive, which is probably the case if you start having trouble making solid contact with the ball or if you start pushing or hooking excessively.

Drill #2: This drill, known as the *Hand-on-the-Shaft Drill,* is designed to allow you to feel the correct initial move down with the lower body as you train your shoulders to stay in position. As I mentioned earlier, one of the major causes of the outside-in downswing is the upper right side and shoulder area moving outward excessively during the initial move down. Sometimes this action can persist, even when trying to use the hips better. This drill allows you to combine both moves together.

Using your driver, stand it vertically in front of your right leg and a distance away from it, so that your left arm is fully extended as you place your open left hand on top of the grip. Now rotate your hips to the left and move your weight onto the left leg. As you do so, swing your right arm under your left while keeping the left arm and driver shaft in their original positions. This will give you the feeling of moving your hips correctly forward while preventing your right shoulder from moving out. You should have the distinct feeling of your right shoulder moving *down*, not *out*, as you execute this drill.

You can also do this drill by swinging your right arm back into a full backswing position with your hips and shoulders turning back accordingly. Now move your left hip laterally about five inches as you rotate your belt buckle approximately 45 degrees toward your target. Again, swing your right arm down and under the extended left. When your right arm goes as far as it can go, your hips will be 45 degrees open to the target, your weight will be fully onto your left leg, and your shoulders will be perfectly square to the target line.

Drill #3: A related drill, sometimes called the *Back-to-the-Target Drill,* is to swing back normally to the top of your backswing. Then initiate a lateral transfer of weight onto your left leg through your hip motion and allow your arms to swing down in response. But while so doing, try to keep the buttons of your shirt facing directly away from the target as long as possible. This is the position they should be in with a 90 degree shoulder turn. You simply want to shift the weight and swing the arms down as far as possible, keeping the shirt buttons, and thus the shoulders, in this position. Again, this prevents the right shoulder from moving the club out in the downswing and you will have the sensation of swinging the clubhead to the ball well from the inside. A 5 or 6 iron would be particularly good for this drill.

The Hand-on-the-Shaft Drill will give you the feeling of moving your hips correctly forward, while preventing your right shoulder from moving out. Here's how it works. Step one: stand a driver vertically in front of your right leg, so that your left arm is fully extended as you place your open left hand on top of the grip. Step two: swing your right arm back into a full backswing position, with your hips and shoulders turning accordingly. It's okay for your left arm to give just a little. Step three: move your left hip laterally about five inches, as you rotate your belt buckle approximately 45 degrees open to the target. As your hips move forward, swing your right arm down under the left. When your right arm goes as far as it can, your hips will be 45 degrees open to the target, your weight will be fully onto your left leg, and your shoulders will be perfectly square to the target.

Pitfall: Allow the forward movement of your hips to drop your right shoulder down naturally. Don't consciously force the movement, which is a common pitfall. When you do this, your shoulder will be going down, but excessively, and your head will be dropping down and to your right as well. Don't allow these motions to happen. Execute the movement while keeping your head up, in its original position, and you will be moving correctly.

Drill #4: Please refer to the 1-2-3 Drill in Chapter 7. As explained, this drill rehearses three aspects of a correct downswing simultaneously. You are working on proper hip motion to begin the downswing, you are allowing the arms to fall downward on plane so you can have the clubhead approach the ball from inside the target line, and you are keeping your wrist cock as the arms begin their initial movement downward. If you do this facing a mirror, as a point of reference, place the back of a light lawn chair about two inches away from your left hip. On the downswing, as you move your left hip laterally forward, it should bump the back of the chair and actually push the back two legs up in the air.

Pitfall: Occasionally players fail to do this drill correctly because they go too fast and try to hit a ball farther than they should. Swing smoothly and relatively slowly. Using a 6 iron, you should be hitting shots only sixty to seventy-five yards. Another problem area is when a student segments the movements too independently and/or makes movements too pronounced. First, your goal is to hit the ball solidly, not far, and feel the relationship of the different movements as you blend them into a nicely sequenced motion. Second, remember the movements are more subtle than pronounced, even though they may feel very different. So be careful not to exaggerate the movements, particularly the lateral hip movement and the downward motion of the right shoulder.

Drill #5: The *Right Foot Back Drill* is a downswing-only drill designed to help you easily feel an inside approach to the ball. Using a 5 iron, address a teed ball with a square stance, ball in center. Now close your stance by moving the right foot back from the stance line at least twelve inches and turn the foot out slightly. As the right foot goes back, the right shoulder *must* be moved back the same amount. You now want to move the ball position back, as well. If you have someone that can do this for you, it is helpful. The ball should go back a good six inches. As the right foot and shoulder go back, be sure to keep your hands and grip end of club forward, so that your club is pointing to the inside of your left leg. Your right arm should be lower then, under your left. This is obviously an extremely closed position. Consequently, you should sense you can make a backswing and then return the clubhead to the ball well from inside the target line. This is exactly what you want to do, sending the ball well to the right initially. To make the ball hook back to the left, sense you are going to contact the ball on its lower inside section with the clubface rotated so closed you think you will hit the ball with the front toe of the clubhead. To accomplish this, you must rotate your left wrist and forearm downward early in the downswing so your clubface will be well closed by impact.

Understand this is a counterdrill for slices. This is not the way you ultimately want to hit golf shots. It is a way to convey to you the feeling of doing the opposite of what you normally do. As you become more and more adept at hitting hooks from the extremely closed position, gradually begin to modify it so the inside approach to the ball becomes less extreme. The goal is to reach the point at which your stance is square and still allows you to have your clubhead approach the target line slightly from the inside and then swing along the line as you contact the ball.

Pitfall: The downside here is that you are compromising a correct takeaway to feel a very inside-out downswing. With the stance and shoulder line exaggeratedly closed at address, the takeaway will naturally be very much to the inside. We accept this as part of the drill procedure, but you do not want to allow this takeaway to infiltrate your normal backswing.

Drill #6: This drill is called the *Low-to-High Drill* and is another sensation drill to feel the clubhead approaching the ball from the inside with the clubface closing vigorously. Use a 5 or 6 iron with a ball on a low tee in the center of your stance. Your grip should be split, all ten fingers on the club. Space your right hand two inches from your left and make sure your grip is relatively strong in both hands, with the vees pointing to right shoulder. This hand positioning is designed to help you accentuate the closing of the clubface through impact.

To execute the drill, take your clubhead from behind the ball and position it back and to your right, so that it is on the ground and on an extension of your stance line. This is your starting position. Your hands will be opposite a point just inside your right knee and your clubhead will be about twelve inches to the right of your right foot. From here, slide your clubhead along the ground to and through the ball, sending it forward. Do not try to swing fast. Swing through smoothly with your arms. However, as you do so, allow your forearms to rotate downward as soon as you initiate the forward motion. The finish of this swing will not be complete. Rather, your arms should be fully extended and angled slightly downward to the right of the target line. They should also be fully rotated, so that the back of the left hand and clubface are facing directly down to the ground. A good procedure is to do this twenty times with a golf ball, then make a full but easy swing trying to execute exactly the same motion. It's okay to use the split grip as you go into your full swing motion, but as the ball begins to hook more and more, gradually work back to your conventional grip.

7. Swing Fault: Inside-Out Downswing

Better players often have worked so hard on not swinging outside-in, they ultimately develop a swing shape that is too much the other way. An interesting facet of this is that as much swing knowledge as this caliber of player may have, such a swing flaw is often exacerbated owing to misdiagnosis of the ball flight and, therefore, the swing that caused it. As mentioned in Chapter 2, the downswing plane plays a major role in the dynamics of the clubface orientation during this segment of the swing. The more inside-out one swings, the more the clubface rotates in a counterclockwise direction. This is because the plane the arms are swinging on promotes a faster rotation of the wrists and forearms. Consequently, the clubface often becomes very closed by the time of impact. And even though the swing path is decidedly to the right and has some degree of influence on the ball's initial flight direction, the extremely closed clubface plays a more dominant role. First, its being closed to the club's path minimizes the amount the ball initially flies to the right. Second, the counterclockwise spin imparted to the ball makes the ball curve left very quickly.

In fact, by the time the golfer's eyes rotate in the through swing and pick up the ball in flight, the ball has already curved left of the target line and continues to curve left even more. But the fact the ball is left of target as soon as the golfer first sees it makes him or her believe the downswing was outside-in. This is often the diagnosis. Result: On the next swing, the golfer tries to swing inside-out even more. The diagnosis was wrong and the correction was wrong. Where the player really gets fooled is if this next shot happens to turn out okay. It corroborates the golfer's initial analysis, and he or she continues on, never really realizing that the downswing plane and path are incorrect.

The player delivers the club well from the inside. At this point in the swing, the clubshaft should be parallel to the pole on the ground.

Cause #1: Often the player will simply take the club back too flat to the inside and leave it on this plane coming down. In such a case, just by correcting the takeaway, the swing dramatically improves; see Swing Fault 1.

Cause #2: The takeaway is good, but as the club moves up to the top, the right elbow raises excessively and/or the right wrist becomes rigid and forceful. As a result, the shaft is forced into an across-the-line position at the top. This means it is pointing to the right and across the target line when it is horizontal to the ground rather than being parallel to it. From such a position, it is very easy for the player to return the club to the ball on too much of an inside path.

Correction: Right hand grip pressure and rigidity in the right wrist must be reduced as the club swings to the top. In addition, the right elbow must be trained to ascend and move away from the right side the correct distance.

Drill: Hold the club in your right hand only and swing up to the top of the backswing with your left hand on your right upper arm. Use your left hand to prevent the right arm from raising excessively. As you do this, allow your right wrist to break back at its base, as it should when both hands are on the club. The wrist cannot be rigid for this to occur. Confirm that the clubshaft is parallel to the target line by either looking in a mirror or asking a friend.

Swing back again with both hands on the club, and duplicate the correct position your club was just in. If the across-the-line position is persistent, move the club up into a laid-off position, aiming the shaft diagonally left of the target when it is horizontal to the ground. Keep your right elbow close to your side as you do this. This certainly is an exaggeration, but if your problem is an extreme one, this is the position you must feel as you hit balls. As you, in fact, begin to make an adjustment to your top-of-backswing position, your downswing plane will change as an automatic response. Continue to feel this top-of-backswing position until you can actually hit left-to-right fades.

Pitfall: A common problem that accompanies this corrective process is that golfers start becoming so involved with their arm swing in the backswing that they start losing some amount of shoulder turn. As the clubshaft goes up to its proper top-of-backswing position, the shoulders must continue to turn 90 degrees. Another problem area is that often students will not stay with their corrective effort long enough, because changing the top-of-backswing position can be so disruptive. Frankly, this takes a little time, so don't abandon your efforts prematurely even if you hit some funny shots at first. A related problem is that golfers usually feel they have made the desired change at the top when, in fact, they have not. If this is the case, and the ball is hit poorly, they will be prone to give up on continuing with the corrective process.

Cause #3: The backswing is good, but on the downswing the hips slide laterally too far toward the target. The arms and club drop too far to the inside with an excessive in-to-out path as a result.

Correction: The left hip lateral motion must be reduced. It must begin to rotate sooner in the downswing. When it does, the right shoulder will move more out and less down as the downswing begins. Consequently, the hands, arms, and club will descend to the ball on plane rather than dropping under it.

Drill #1: Previously, I described some drills using a light lawn chair to monitor hip movement. Here's another one. Facing a mirror, take your address position with any club. Face the back of the light chair toward your left hip and leg, but no more than two inches away. Make some practice swings. As you swing down, allow your left hip to move left enough to contact the chair, but not push its back forward so that the back two legs of the chair come off the ground. The left hip moves only *to* the chair as it rotates on around to the left. If your left leg has previously been too bent at the knee, you will quickly realize it must firm up and straighten to cause the left hip to rotate more and slide less.

Drill #2: A related drill is to perform this hip motion swinging with your left arm only. Place your right hand on your left shoulder, and as your left hip rotates to the left in the through swing, push your left shoulder back in the same direction. You should get a strong sense of your shoulders and chest opening up to the target, just as your hips are doing, as you swing through.

Do these drills often and relate to the sensations you experience. As you begin to hit balls, duplicate these movements as best you can until you begin to hit left-to-right fades.

Address position with back of chair two inches away from left hip.

If the left hip moves too far laterally, the back two chair legs will elevate off the ground.

Pitfall: Be careful not to spin your hips so much in the downswing you fail to move your weight up onto your left leg. Also, be careful not to move the right shoulder, arm, and club out so much on the downswing you begin to overdo it. Let your golf ball be your guide. If you start hitting unsolid pulls and/or big slices, you have gone too far.

Cause #4: The backswing is good, but the hands, arms, and club simply drop too vertically at the initiation of the downswing, resulting in a too inside-out path through the ball. Postimpact, the arms swing out and away from the body excessively, resulting in an upswing that is too vertical and a body finish that is less than complete. Hooks, blocks to the right with the driver, and fat and thin shots result.

Correction: The hand line down must be more on the proper diagonal line, as discussed in Chapter 4. Certainly, the drills already discussed that relate to the hip and shoulder motion apply here. But we can also see marked improvement focusing just on the shape of the arm swing, as influenced by the hand line, as we swing the club down and through.

Drill #1: An excellent practice procedure is simply to rehearse swinging the club down to Position 5, identified in Chapter 4. At this position, the shaft is horizontal to the ground, parallel to the foot line, and on the toe line. When the club is coming down too far under the plane, the shaft would be angled back at this point. Set up to a teed ball with a 5 iron, swing back to the top, rehearse this downswing position twice, then hit your shot. This is similar in execution to the 1-2-3 Drill. Keep hitting shots until the ball starts straight at your target and flies straight, rather than right of target or with excessive hook.

Pitfall: As you swing your club and arms down, do it slowly, both in your rehearsals and when you actually hit the ball. Also, make sure your hips, knees, and legs are active as you rehearse down. It is common to start standing dead legged as you focus on what your arms and club are doing.

Drill #2: This is a simple drill to work on your downswing by focusing on your through swing. Place an intermediate target in front of your golf ball about four yards down your target line. Set up to a ball on the ground with your driver. Without making any backswing, push the ball forward to the *left* of your intermediate target. This can be a headcover or any object that clearly gives you a point of reference. As your arms swing forward, rotate your left hip to the left and allow your weight to shift forward onto your left leg. You should feel your hands swinging much more left than you are used to. They should be swinging close to your left hip before going up. Your right arm should be in close contact with your upper right chest area, not separating out and away from your body. This gives you a wonderful sensation of how your arms should be swinging and your body moving to propel a golf ball straight or slightly left of target, as opposed to the right.

Drill #3: Another good feel—and visual—drill is to see that you can have your hands and butt end of club swing more left than you had been before, but still have the club approach from the inside. Although the other drills help you sense a more cut action through the ball, it's important to note that they are designed only to help you find the proper degree of inside approach you should have in your swing. If you are too inside-out, this approach has become too exaggerated. Using a longer club, such as a driver, choke down on the shaft a good eighteen to twenty inches so that the length of shaft above your hands can rest along your left side. Make a miniature swinging motion, swinging the shaft back to parallel to the ground. Notice as you swing forward and as the clubhead approaches an imaginary target line, the grip end of the club is moving left, away from it. This is good feedback, conceptually, so that you understand your hands can swing more to the left postimpact and still have the clubhead approach from the inside as it should.

Pitfall: The one major problem the very accomplished player runs into when trying to swing less inside out is, at first, swinging out too much coming down. Both the hands and the clubhead move out excessively in the downswing, resulting in pulls or weak cuts. The next stage has the player, realizing the clubhead has started to come out too much, move it back closer to the correct plane, if not on it. However, the hands and the hand line continue to move out excessively, even though the player has managed to manipulate the clubhead onto a more acceptable plane. The result is a shaft that has moved up into too vertical a position at impact. Because the hands moved *out* too much coming down, they are *up* too much at impact, much higher than they were at address. The clubhead may be approaching on an acceptable path; but because the hands and grip end of the club are so out of position, the hands and wrists cannot possibly release correctly. This results in severe blocks and overall poor shots.

Drill #4: An excellent drill procedure for this problem—and for the arms swinging out excessively away from the body owing to the overly inside-out downswing—is to place a shaft in the ground just above and just left of the shaft of the club you are swinging. Insert this shaft at the same angle as your club in the address position. Make some slow practice swings, making sure not to hit the angled shaft in the ground as you move forward in your through swing. As you swing down, you should feel your hands moving more downward as your clubhead is moving more outward—hands in, clubhead out. When done correctly, you should be able to return the shaft of the club you are swinging to a position at impact that duplicates its position at address, grip end and hands no higher. If so, you can then continue forward and swing under the angled shaft in the ground without any part of your club hitting it. As you get the feel for this motion, gradually increase the speed of your swing until you can incorporate the corrected movement into a normal speed swing.

Reflections and the Lessons I've Learned

Helping golfers improve their swings and shot-making skills so they can shoot lower scores and enjoy the game more is what a big part of my life is all about. Yes, I've been lucky to have been exposed to the knowledge of former great teachers, such as Claude Harmon, the father of the Harmon boys, including Dick when he works with tour players, and Butch, who now teaches Tiger Woods. But the conversations I have on a daily basis with today's teachers, most notably Henry Young, my golf academy director, and friends Jim Flick, Jim McLean, Randy Smith, Bob Toski, David Leadbetter, and Jim Ferree, really allow me to improve my skills. In fact, I'm sure some of the information I have shared with you in this book could not have been put forth so clearly if not for the knowledge and insights that have been passed on to me over the years. Frankly, though, my learning experiences go much deeper and involve others, such as my parents and tour players. Let me share some of my experiences.

Hands-on teacher David Leadbetter is an instructor I admire a great deal.

From My Parents

As a junior player, I was very fortunate to be supported by both of my parents. They encouraged me to play golf but never pushed me into becoming the greatest golfer who ever lived. They knew it had to come from me. Their supportive, carefree attitude allowed me to grow more freely. I enjoyed having fun, practicing, and competing. Whether I won a junior event or lost, my parents were always there. I also played other sports as well; that balance was good for me.

Coordination and competition teaches many things to kids. Too many parents today expect their sons and daughters to perform at high levels. They need to give them the space to develop good skills and generally have fun playing, or participating in a group lesson program. My advice to parents is to utilize good teachers who can teach your children the basics of the setup and the fundamentals of the swing. Unless you have qualified knowledge, don't try correcting their swing yourself.

I remember a fellow junior state championship competitor, saying, "If I don't finish strong and in top 5, my dad is going to be livid and upset. I will probably have to stay in my room all weekend." All I could think was, how lucky I had it, and how unfortunate my friend was because of his situation at home. Later, that talented junior left the game and to my knowledge he hasn't played since. A very sad story for sure. I still remember it when I see parents pressuring their kids. My parents never pressured me; they just supported me and let me develop. That's the philosophy I've adopted with my son, Hunter.

From My Brother

My brother Andy taught me that competition is healthy. Competition is a test and barometer which teaches us to dig down into our souls and work hard to try to be the best we possibly can.

Andy also taught me the importance of hard work. There is no substitute for the proper work ethic, and no shortcuts exist. Having said that, it's important that you practice the right things. If not, you will reach a very different destination than the one you planned to reach. In short, you will be taking a backward step.

Whether you are a beginner or a veteran player, always set goals and test yourself, to better measure yourself. You don't always have to participate in a Nassau bet. Competing against the course should be enough to make you practice harder, to lower your handicap. I do believe that you should play with better players, as I so immensely enjoyed doing with my brother Andy when I was young. This allowed me to stay focused on one thing, scoring lower than my opponent. If your goals aren't that high, just try to enjoy the game.

From Mike Hulbert and Coach Hal Morrison

I attended East Tennessee University. One of my fellow golf team members was Mike Hulbert, who now plays on the PGA Tour. Mike's swing was unorthodox, but efficient. Like Coach Morrison, Mike believes that a swing doesn't have to look pretty or be technically perfect to work. As I learned, you can hit good golf shots, with your desired ball flight and trajectory, even with an unorthodox or visually unappealing swing, provided you deliver the club solidly to the ball at impact. Are you consistent—and I mean consistently good—with your method?

From Don Kotnik

As a young professional, I also worked for Don Kotnik at the Toledo Country Club, in Ohio. Don taught me the value of being the best at whatever you do, whether it was playing, teaching, or providing the best service to the members. Don and I enjoyed creating junior programs. He always believed in me, and he had high expectations of me. I always liked that because he cared and would do anything to help me. He believed that a person should utilize their strengths, so he let me teach for many hours during the day. I am indebted to him for not keeping me cooped up in the pro shop, and for allowing me to learn so much during that key period of my life.

From Walker Inman

At age twenty-one, I worked for Walker Inman, the pro at Scioto Country Club, the course that Jack Nicklaus grew up on. Walker realized the importance of playing and practicing. When we played early morning rounds of golf, we were very competitive. Walker would say, "We pushed one another." Our competitive matches were healthy because we were able to think about scoring rather than the intricacies of the swing. Make sure that you give yourself time to play, because there's no experience like course experience.

From Lee Janzen

I've been teaching Lee Janzen since he was thirteen years old, when he came to me with high tops and curly hair. Back then, Lee had a fiery temper. Later, in college, he learned the hard way that you play better when you use your anger in a positive way. That mature attitude has certainly served him well on the PGA Tour.

Although I've played my share of pressure-filled matches, Lee always reinforced in me the importance of staying in the present, no matter what the circumstances. This attitude helped Lee win many tournaments, most notably the 1993 United States Open and the 1995 Players Championship.

From Rocco Mediate

Years ago, Rocco came to me to change his swing, to get better. He did improve and became a better ball striker. In fact, the bottom of his swing arc is superior. My goal was to work with what he had. After a couple of tour wins with a long putter, he questioned whether he should go back to the short putter. This doubt took away from his earlier years of excitement with the long putter. Whether it's a swing or putting, you need to believe in yourself. Moreover, as you drive to be the best, don't

Rocco Mediate putted best with a long putter.

forget you possess certain qualities that have made you what you are. *Lesson:* Don't be afraid of change, if you feel that the potential benefits are greater than your current results.

From Billy Andrade

In the early 1990s, Billy Andrade wanted a teacher who would help him without totally revamping his swing. He found out from Lee and Rocco that I was not a method teacher, so he chose me as his instructor. Billy was quite new on tour and he wanted to hit the ball longer.

Billy is of rather small stature, only five foot eight. He soon proved to me, once again, that you don't have to be tall and muscular to hit the ball solidly. He was flexible and wiry and deceptively long. He recently won a long drive contest you may have seen on TV.

On the lesson tee, he told me that the hook shot gave him more distance, but cost him accuracy. Hitting fairways is what's all important on tee shots, so I worked with him to hit a left-to-right power-fade drive. Not only did this shot allow him to keep the ball in the short grass off the tee, it allowed him to hit more greens in regulation and score better as a result. The fade swing also felt more natural, and gave Billy the ability to swing along the target line more consistently. He now drives the ball better due to his swing becoming rounder.

In working with Billy, I learned something very important about the teaching process. Because Billy is a feel player, he does not respond well to instructional terminology or words. Billy is an image learner, meaning that he learns more quickly when shown a movement. He doesn't like being told about it. He also responds better to drills, so I don't even bother explaining the complexities of the swing to Billy. For example, when Billy falls into a slump, it's usually because he swings his arms on a very exaggerated steep plane. To remedy this problem, I have him flatten out his plane by hitting shots off sidehill lies, with the ball above his feet or have him make baseball swings promoting a level turn, which is a nice opposite for him. Try to determine what type of learner you are, then find a pro that teaches your way of learning.

Billy Andrade swings more freely when he's shown what to do rather than told what to do. He doesn't like to think about technique; he likes to feel it.

From Jack Nicklaus

In working with Jack Nicklaus, I learned the vital importance of observing and listening intently to a student before making a change to his or her technique.

After watching Jack hit hundreds of practice balls, and studying his swing on video for hours and hours, I noticed that a steep angle of approach was causing his quick-left shots. By encouraging him to widen his arc, which allowed him to make a deeper turn, his plane became more shallow. This swing change also allowed him to swing from inside to along the target line, rather than out to right field with a steep angle.

Before you make a personal change to your existing swing, watch your action on video with a professional. Video analysis is an excellent teaching tool, yet it has its place. Looking at video too often can make

When playing club championship matches, take a lesson from Jack Nicklaus. Under pressure, he mentally blocks out the gallery and lets the situation excite him rather than intimidate him.

you too picky about your swing. You may also lose your ability to feel things. Further, when a student is playing well, I don't like showing video. It's time to play golf, not analyze.

Here are some other things I learned from Jack. When you practice, try to feel your swing in a flow, rather than think about each individual movement. When Jack feels weight on his front left toe, he knows he's sliding his lower body on the downswing. When he feels a "flashy" feeling of the hands in the impact zone, he knows he's swinging too much from inside to out. *Your lesson:* Learn to get proper feedback through feel. Your feel can lie to you, but once you have acquired the proper feel, remember it and take notes in a journal.

Out on the course, Jack keeps his swing thoughts to a minimum. Once again, he lets feel link him to a smooth swing rhythm for the day. He also allows pressure situations to excite him rather than intimidate him. Every club-level golfer can gain from following this advice.

One chief reason Vijay Singh's swing is so consistent is because he practices intelligently. It's the quality of your practice that counts, not the quantity of balls you hit.

From Vijay Singh

The one lesson I learned from tour player Vijay Singh involves practice. It's not the quantity of balls you hit, but the quality of your practice that matters most. Always practice with a purpose. Don't merely beat balls. Vijay is very strong physically, and this helps him to practice for long hours. Many of you would practice better if you put quality before quantity. There is nothing worse than watching an amateur who is a tired practicer. The reason is, this is when new bad faults creep in.

From David Duval

Obviously talented, David possesses an unorthodox yet very efficient swing style. His stronger grip and shut face match up perfectly to his body motion. David needs to always stay with what he has to control his shot shape and trajectory. If he mixes the wrong thoughts that are not compatible to his style, he will struggle. *Your Lesson is:* Know your style, and know there is sensitivity with swing changes.

From Phil Mickelson

Phil Mickelson possesses the touch of a magician, maybe the best who has ever lived. The reason Phil is such a short game wizard is that, during his youthful days, he practiced hitting hundreds of shots out of a variety of lies with a variety of clubs. Such practice habits allow you to develop a very versatile and creative shotmaking repertoire, and to score better out on the course.

During his practice sessions, Phil works the ball deliberately in different directions to keep his swing in check. Try this, and your feel will improve, plus you'll be able to identify your swing faults more easily. It also helps elimanate overly mechanical thoughts. Phil is a world class guy who will continue to win many events, including majors.

From Tom Kite

Tom Kite has been criticized for skipping from teacher to teacher and trying new things practically every week. That's not true. He knows what to do and merely appreciates a good set of eyes. Tom listens to varying views on technique, but he never makes a switch unless he believes he can easily incorporate a specific movement into his existing swing. Its important to keep your swing in check. Become educated about your swing, so you can weed out the information that you do not need.

Bernhard Langer proves that trying something new, such as an unorthodox "claw grip," can help you hole more putts.

From Bernhard Langer

The phrase "Where there's a will there's a way" certainly applies to Bernhard Langer. He's had the yips three times during his career. However, rather than give up, he solved his problem each time by having the courage to try a different putting technique. First, he putted cross-handed. Next, he let much of the putter shaft rest against the inside of his left forearm and then grasped his arm and the shaft with his right hand. Finally, he started using a long putter. *Your Lesson:* Don't ever give up, and continue to look at positive things.

From Bill Glasson

Bill Glasson is a winner who has fought through extensive injuries. He truly is the definition of what dedication and the will to win is all about. Billy is intelligent and can really play. *Your Lesson:* Believe you can do anything, and use your internal drive to become better.

From Gary Nicklaus

Gary Nicklaus is a very talented young man, who has done a good job handling his position as son of the greatest golfer that ever lived. Humble and kind, whether or not he becomes the player I think he can be, he has succeeded as far as I am concerned. He's a good person, which is first and foremost. I look forward to his success.

I hope you have enjoyed these reflections and lessons. I hope, too, that you will let this book serve as your guide to solving specific problems you may experience in your golfing life.

In your quest to improve, be sure to identify your swing weaknesses and strive to eliminate them. Know that this game is difficult for everyone. Know, too, however, that improvement is attainable. Enjoy good shots and the company you keep on the course. Be competitive, but set realistic goals. Watch carefully and listen to others, but develop your own swing through intelligent evaluation. Feel your swing, so you can repeat it more easily or trace a fault quickly. Most of all, have fun.

Good luck, friends.

Rick Smith is Director of Golf at Treetops Resort in Gaylord, Michigan, and hosts the *Rick Smith Signature* series on ESPN-TV. An award-winning golf-course designer, Smith is a corporate spokesperson for TopFlite and the Ford Motor Company. He is also on the Pro-Panel of *Golf Digest* magazine.

Rick Smith Enterprises

P.O. Box 578

Gaylord, Michigan 49734